W9-AVM-966

Wild Truth Journal

DARES FROM JESUS

50 Truth and Dare Challenges for Junior Highers

Wild Truth Journal

DARES FROM JESUS

50 Truth and Dare Challenges for Junior Highers

Mark Oestreicher

ZONDERVAN™

YS Youth Specialties

10 20 P·R·E·S·S

Wild Truth Bible Journal—Dares from Jesus: 50 truth and dare challenges for junior highers

Copyright © 2002 by Youth Specialties

Youth Specialties Books, 300 S. Pierce St., El Cajon, CA 92020, are published by Zondervan, 5300 Patterson Ave. S.E., Grand Rapids, MI 49530.

Unless otherwise indicated, all Scripture quotations are taken from the *Holy Bible: New International Version* (North America Edition). Copyright © 1973, 1978, 1984 by International Bible Society. Used by permission of Zondervan Publishing House.

All rights reserved. No part of this publication may be reproduced, stored in a retrieval system, or transmitted in any form or by any means—electronic, mechanical, photocopy, recording, or any other—except for brief quotations in printed reviews, without the prior permission of the publisher.

Edited by Rick Marschall and Linda Bannan
Illustrations by Krieg Barrie
Design by Tom Gulotta
Production assistance by Sarah Sheerin

Printed in the United States of America

03 04 05 06 07/ CH / 10 9 8 7 6 5 4 3

DARING CONTENTS

DEDICATION

To my way-cool nephews and nieces: Kirsten, Zachary, Shana, Jacob, Rachel, Sara, Lydia, Hannah and Julia. I'm so glad that all of you have taken the dare to follow Jesus!

ACKNOWLEDGEMENTS

I'm always in a debt of gratitude to the most creative person I know: Todd Temple, my *Wild Truth* partner. Todd came up with the *Dares From Jesus* idea, and he researched all the scripture passages. The product department staff at Youth Specialties—Urb, Sarah, Roni, and Rick —is truly an amazing group. Thanks again for graciously straddling the balance of coworkers and development team when it comes to my books. And I could never be involved in this writing ministry were it not for the support of my amazing friend/lover/partner/bride Jeannie.

TRUTH OR DARE!

Everyone played this game as a kid, right? Maybe you still play it with your friends sometimes. When it's your turn, you choose whether you want Truth—which means you have to answer *any* question with complete honesty; or Dare—which means you're given a physical challenge to complete.

Maybe you're at least somewhat like me: I'm really motivated by dares. If someone challenges me, I hate to ignore it. It bugs me to not complete a dare.

That probably explains why I busted into another school to sing a love song in the classroom of a girl I liked.

That probably explains why I was always the one to drink the sludge in that skit where a bunch of people all use the same glass of water to brush their teeth and gargle.

And it probably explains why I figured out that I could snort dental floss up my nose and cough it out my mouth and gross people out by "flossing my nose."

Dares probably account for why I've done most of the weird and stupid things in my life!

Many people don't realize it, but the Bible—especially the teachings of Jesus in the gospels—is full of dares. In fact (this is totally cool), it's the perfect Truth *and* Dare. When Jesus speaks, he almost always says something like: "Here's the truth, and here's what I dare you to do about it."

That's what this book is all about. If you want to be a disciple of Jesus (a Jesus-follower), then it's time for the ultimate version of Truth or Dare. Are you willing to take the dare?

note to parents and youth leaders

First let me say thanks for taking an interest in the spiritual life of a young teen. You are a rare and wonderful person, and I wish I could take you to Starbucks and buy you a Grande Caramel Macchiato while lavishing praise and encouragement all over you.

If you want this book to be most helpful to the teen(s) you care about, you should understand a few things:

- First, this book is *best* used when students have an opportunity to complete a lesson (or two or three) on their own, and then debrief it with an adult. When students discuss the Truth and the Dares, their understanding and the lesson's impact is increased—as well as the likelihood that the teens will actually follow through with the dare.

- Certainly this debriefing can be orchestrated in many effective ways, but I've greatly enjoyed meeting regularly with a few students in a very small group. I complete the lessons on my own, and the group becomes an effective cross-pollinator as kids challenge each other and me.

- Also be aware that this book has two companion books of Bible lessons, called *Wild Truth Bible Lessons: Dares from Jesus* and *Wild Truth Bible Lessons: Dares from Jesus 2*. Each of these books takes 12 lessons from this journal and develops them into full-blown youth group sessions with crowd breakers, teaching times, small group activities, and applications. The Bible lessons and the journals can be very effective when used together.

- Finally, this is the third in a trilogy of *Wild Truth Journals* for junior highers. The first—*Wild Truth Journal*—illustrates 50 life lessons based on characters from the Bible. The second—*Wild Truth Journal: Pictures of God*—looks at 50 self-portraits of God in scripture, then helps young teens identify and develop those characteristics in themselves. The three journals (and their accompanying *Bible Lessons* books) make a good three-year (or three-semester) cycle.

I wish God's richest blessings on you and your ministry (in a church setting or your home) with young teens!

Your partner in ministry,

Mark Oestreicher

Turn On The Lights!

Read: Matthew 5:14-16

WHAT JESUS SAID

Jesus said:
"No one lights a lamp and then puts it under a _____."

    a. slab of cheddar
    b. poodle
    c. bowl
    d. cone of silence

In these verses Jesus uses "light" to talk about:

    a. candles
    b. good stuff we do
    c. lighting stuff on fire

WHAT JESUS MEANT

Putting a lamp under a _____ (What was it again?) is similar to: (Circle all that are similar.)

Putting an air horn in a sound proof room.

Placing a piece of the world's best chocolate into a cup of vinegar.

Sending a teenager into a room full of giant squid.

Giving a wristwatch to someone who has no idea of time.

Giving color samples to a blind person.

"Let your light shine before men" means:

JESUS WAS TALKING TO ME

Rate these teens on the "light scale":

1 ——————————————— 5 ——————————————— 10

under a bowl!   dim, but visible   it's a searchlight!

Erin spent some of her hard-earned baby-sitting money to buy a birthday present for a girl in school who doesn't have any friends.

_____

Billy made a very tough choice today: he picked up trash in the park while his buddies were all playing hoops.

_____

Jase loves it when all the lights are on in the house. It bugs his mom, but he's always running around turning on all the switches.

_____

Brainstorm four ways a teen can be a light shining on a hill:

1.

2.

3.

DARE THE TRUTH

4.

Jesus Christ Power and Light Company
Light Contract

On _____ (Choose a day this week.), I, _____ (Write your name.), will be

"light" by _____

_____ (Write the good deed you will do.).

_____ signature

Get Past It!

Read: Matthew 5:21-26

WHAT JESUS SAID

Jesus seems pretty bugged by people who carry _____.
- a. penguins
- b. grudges
- c. guns
- d. pocket change

It seems he's also not too thrilled when we ignore people we've _____.
- a. paid
- b. hurt
- c. seen
- d. shared cheesecake with

WHAT JESUS MEANT

A definition of reconciliation: (Check one)
- ❑ to bring back together, as in: "Sorry about that, let's be reconciled."
- ❑ to look back at being silly, as in: "Ha, ha! That was so reconsilly!"
- ❑ to put together, as in: "I'm going to reconcile this bologna and this cheese."

Why do you think Jesus cares if we get along with people?
(No easy answers here—think before you write!)

JESUS WAS TALKING TO ME

What reconciliation might mean for me... (Check all that apply)
- ❏ getting back together with my old girlfriend or boyfriend
- ❏ saying I'm sorry and asking forgiveness
- ❏ pointing out to someone how much they've hurt me
- ❏ forgiving someone I've been ticked with
- ❏ stopping this lesson *right now* and calling someone on the phone
- ❏ demanding someone ask for forgiveness from me

If you were to spring into action and do what you need to do to fix a hurt relationship you have with someone right now (really, right this minute—well, after you answer this question), what would it look like? How would it affect your day?

What are some of the results of not reconciling with people?

DARE THE TRUTH

Jesus said to do it NOW! Are you willing to take the dare?

Whom I need to reconcile with	When, and how, I'll reconcile

GO! DO IT NOW!!

Rule or Be Ruled!

Read: Matthew 5:27-30

WHAT JESUS **SAID**

Wow! This is some pretty radical stuff! If you take this passage at face value, which body parts would you have to hack off or gouge out? (C'mon, be honest!)

- ❏ eye
- ❏ leg
- ❏ hand
- ❏ mouth
- ❏ um, private stuff
- ❏ brain (ouch!)
- ❏ spleen
- ❏ ear

WHAT JESUS **MEANT**

Do you think Jesus really wants you to get crazy and hack yourself to pieces?

- ❏ Yes, and I'm also on my way to the nut house right now.
- ❏ No, I understand that Jesus sometimes speaks in exaggerated ways to make his point.

Who or what makes you sin? (Circle all that apply, but—hint, hint—there's really only one correct answer.)

the devil	my spleen
the temptation	someone else
sin? what sin?	me and only me!

JESUS WAS TALKING TO ME

How much control do you have of your body? (Add a needle on this meter to show your answer.)

I've got *some* control

I've got *no* control   I'm in *total* control

Here's the deal: Jesus says ya got a choice. Rule your body ("Body, I am the king of you! And I am in authority!"). Or let your body rule you ("Oooh, you're just so overpowering that I can do nothing but what you urge me to do!"). So, what does "ruling your body" look like for a teen?

DARE THE TRUTH

What parts of your body
almost seem like they have a mind and will of their own sometimes? (Yup, this is a little uncomfortable to talk and write about—but don't be a wimp, check all that apply.)

❑ my eyes (what I look at)   ❑ my hands (what I touch)   ❑ my feet (where I go)
❑ my mind (what I think about)   ❑ my mouth (what I say)   ❑ other:

Now go back and circle the one body part that rules you the most. What will it take to reestablish your "rule" over this part of your body this week?

Write a prayer to Jesus to ask him for strength to follow through on this plan:

Enough Said

Read: Matthew 5:33-37

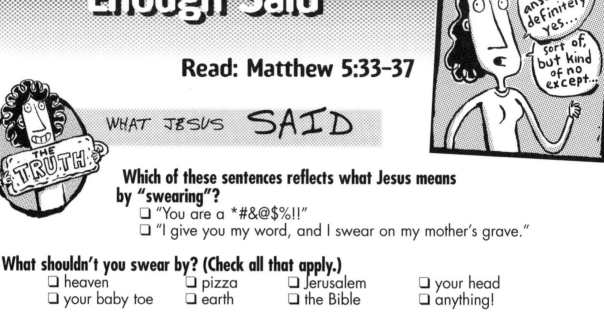

WHAT JESUS **SAID**

Which of these sentences reflects what Jesus means by "swearing"?
- ❏ "You are a *#&@$%!!"
- ❏ "I give you my word, and I swear on my mother's grave."

What shouldn't you swear by? (Check all that apply.)
- ❏ heaven
- ❏ your baby toe
- ❏ pizza
- ❏ earth
- ❏ Jerusalem
- ❏ the Bible
- ❏ your head
- ❏ anything!

According to Jesus...

Yes should = _____   No should = _____

WHAT JESUS **MEANT**

Which of these best defines "integrity"?
- ❏ You can count on me to lie.
- ❏ You can believe what I say to be true, and it won't change.
- ❏ I'm a good person.

Why does Jesus care if we have integrity, if people can count on our words to be true?

JESUS WAS TALKING TO ME

Write about a time when you made a promise and broke it:

Write about a time when someone made a promise to you and then broke it:

In the verse you read today, Jesus makes it clear that we shouldn't bother backing up our promises with a bunch of "in the name ofs" and "on a stack ofs." People should just be able to believe that when we say something, it's the truth. This sounds simple. Why isn't it?

DARE THE TRUTH

Choose the dare that makes the most sense here:

- ❏ I, _____ (name), swear on a stack of Bibles not to swear on a stack of Bibles.
- ❏ I, _____ (name), promise, with my fingers crossed behind my back, to be a person of integrity.
- ❏ I, _____ (name), will let my yes be yes, and my no be no. God, help me to be honest with my words.

Is there anything else you need to do this week to clean up some yes's that were really no's, or the other way around?

Take Them In Pairs

Read: Matthew 5:38–42

WHAT JESUS SAID

If someone pokes you in the eye, you should:
- ❏ say, "Praise-a-luia! Thank you, Jesus!"
- ❏ let 'em poke you again, in the other eye
- ❏ say, "you are a mean little person, you…you…eye-poker!"
- ❏ poke 'em back
- ❏ say "ow"

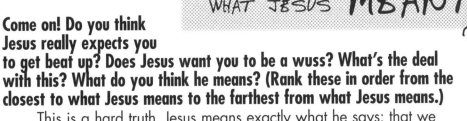

WHAT JESUS MEANT

Come on! Do you think Jesus really expects you to get beat up? Does Jesus want you to be a wuss? What's the deal with this? What do you think he means? (Rank these in order from the closest to what Jesus means to the farthest from what Jesus means.)

____ This is a hard truth. Jesus means exactly what he says: that we shouldn't fight back or try to defend ourselves.

____ Jesus doesn't want you to be a punching bag, but he wants you to forgive people who hurt you.

____ Jesus just doesn't like fighting. You can get revenge in lots of other ways.

____ Trying to get back at people—if they hurt you physically or in some other way—is a waste of time, and doesn't show love. Jesus is all about love.

So really, if a guy socked Jesus in the stomach, what do you think Jesus would have done? What would he have said?

JESUS WAS TALKING TO ME

This is a hard-core dare! Easy dares aren't much of a dare, really. But this one goes totally against what we want to do!

True story

Nathan learned a form of martial arts as a missionary kid in Africa—and got really, really good at it. Now, he lives in the Chicago area and attending a public school, and he's been getting beat up by a group of guys every day on his way home. He never fights back, even though he could take on all of the guys at one time and beat them. How crazy is Nathan?

He's an idiot! | He doesn't really understanding what Jesus meant. | That's real courage—choosing not to fight back!

True story

Erika is tall for her age, and a group of students at school have started calling her names like: telephone pole, beanstalk, and tall freak. They've made it a game to come up with new names for her. Erika would love to fight back. She's way smarter then they are, and she could come up with some great names to shoot back. But she doesn't. She's trying to respond with a simple "hi" and a smile. Then she tries to silently pray for the kid who called her a name. She's found that when she prays for them, God takes away some of her anger. How crazy is Erika?

She *is* a freak! | It's nice that she prays for them, but she doesn't have to smile. | Wow—Erika's my hero!

Who has hurt you lately (physically or with insults or something else)?

DARE THE TRUTH

What did they do to you?

What would you like to do to this person?

What will you do—to accept this tough dare from Jesus?

18

Act Like They're Not

Read: Matthew 5:43–48

WHAT JESUS **SAID**

Which custom license plate would Jesus have on this car? (Sound 'em out, then circle one or two!)

Why does Jesus say we should love our enemies? (Check one)
- ❏ Because Jesus likes to say things that are impossible
- ❏ So people will call us religious freaks
- ❏ 'Cause we're God's children, and God loves everyone
- ❏ Because sugar and spice makes everything nice

WHAT JESUS **MEANT**

What does it look like to love an enemy? How is that possible?

19

JESUS WAS TALKING TO ME

Which of these are ways teens could love their enemies? (Check all that apply.)
- ❑ pray for them
- ❑ pray for them to move away (maybe to another planet)
- ❑ do something nice for them without them knowing you did it
- ❑ don't seek revenge if they do or say something mean
- ❑ say nice things about them to someone else
- ❑ forgive them
- ❑ try to think of something positive about them
- ❑ T.P. their house in the middle of the night
- ❑ give them some cabbage

Rank these kinds of enemies from "easiest to love" (1) to "hardest to love" (5):

____ an enemy you've never met before—you just know you don't like them (They don't even know who you are.)

____ someone who's said really hurtful things to you and is mean to you all the time

____ someone who's hurt you physically or taken something from you

____ someone who's been mean to someone you love

____ someone you don't really know—they're just part of a group of people you don't like

Follow these instructions to take the dare:

DARE THE TRUTH

1. Choose one of the enemy categories from the last question. Put a star next to it.
2. Write the name of a person here who fits that description (if you know a name). _____.
3. Choose a way to love this enemy from the first question on this page. Put a star next to it.
4. Write here when and how you'll carry out this act:

Shhhh!

Read: Matthew 6:1-4

...and we thanketh thee for thy mercy though we deserveth it not-eth and furthermore-eth...

WHAT JESUS **SAID**

THE TRUTH

In this verse, Jesus kind of assumes you are: (Check one, and only one.)
- ❏ reading your Bible
- ❏ giving money to help the poor
- ❏ named Ferdinand
- ❏ cleaning your bedroom

Most young teens don't (do the last answer). Be honest: are you? (Circle an answer.)

Yes   No

But that's not the real point of the truth, is it? Jesus' point is: (Choose one.)
- ❏ When you give to the poor, give lots and lots and lots (C'mon, you cheapo!)
- ❏ When you give to the poor, don't make a big honkin' deal about it, hoping to get lots of attention.
- ❏ When you give to the poor, make sure they don't use it to buy alcohol.
- ❏ If your name is Ferdinand, Jesus loves you.

WHAT JESUS **MEANT**

THE TRUTH

This is really about more than just giving to the poor. What does Jesus want from us? (Choose one.)
- ❏ To not make a big deal about *any* giving—giving money, giving time or resources, serving.
- ❏ To make sure everyone you know is aware of everything you give—make posters even!
- ❏ To feel really sorry for poor people.
- ❏ if your name is Ferdinand, consider going by the nickname "Nando."

21

JESUS WAS TALKING TO ME

It seems that you have two options when you give or serve, and they're opposites. Draw a line between the two opposite attitudes in each list that reflect what Jesus is talking about.

Give or serve as an offering to God, and do not care if anyone else knows. ○

Give lots. ○

Tie your left arm behind your back when you give. ○

○ Give little.

○ Shh! Don't tell your left arm what you're doing! It's a secret!

○ Give or serve so everyone will think you're a great kid, and ruin the point of giving or serving.

What ways can junior highers give? (Brainstorm at least six ways. Remember, they don't all have to involve money.)

1.

2.

3.

4.

5.

6.

DARE THE TRUTH

Here's the big dare for the day...ready?
Give some money (your money—maybe that means you have to do something to earn some first!) to the poor or to an organization that works with the poor (your church can probably help you find one, if you don't know of one), and don't tell anyone what you did! (You might have to be a bit sneaky to pull this off—like you might have to give your mom some money and ask her to write a check for you, but don't tell her what it's for.)

❑ I accept this dare!   ❑ I'm a wimp; I don't accept this dare.

Go Undercover

Read: Matthew 6:5–8

 WHAT JESUS **SAID**

In the last dare ("Shh!"), Jesus challenged you to give without trying to get attention. This dare is kind of like it (Jesus really doesn't want us to do stuff that should be for him just to get attention for ourselves). This dare is about:

_____.

Where does the J-man suggest you go when you carry out this action?

 WHAT JESUS **MEANT**

Which of these phrases sums up what Jesus was saying? (You can choose more than one if you want.)

❑ Say it; don't spray it.　　❑ Keep it simple, stupid.
❑ Eat your vegetables.　　❑ Just talk to him.
❑ Preach it, baby!

Does this mean you shouldn't ever pray out loud, like in your youth group? (Underline one.)

DUH, NO　　　　　I dunno　　　　　Gee, I guess so

JESUS WAS TALKING TO ME

Which of these is the best kind of prayer for praying out loud in church?

❑ O, great God in heaven, we beseech thee to have mercy on us. We cometh before thee and ask for thy powerful eye to take notice of us lowly worms. We thanketh thee for all thy bountiful blessings, o Lord. Ameneth.

❑ God, thanks for loving us. Thanks for forgiving us.

Which one of these teens understands this dare?

❑ Jenna loves to pray—she knows it's her lifeline to God. But Jenna knows she's *good* at praying (at least that's what all the adults in her church say). So she looks for every opportunity to pray out loud in church, 'cause people always say the nicest things to her afterward.

❑ Milton thinks praying in school is a big deal, and he has been a strong voice in the arguments about school prayer in his community. Every day he stands by his locker before class and prays out loud for his school, his classmates, and the legal system. Milton thinks of his prayers as a protest of sorts.

❑ Trina talks to God constantly—all day long. But most of the time no one would know it, 'cause she's just talking to Jesus silently. But her favorite times of prayer are when she goes home after school, shuts the door to her room, and pours her heart out—out loud—to God.

Circle the correct words:

Let's make sure this is totally clear! Jesus wants me to pray [*all the time, once in a while, at church*]. In fact, 1 Thessalonians 5:17 says, "pray [*hard, continually, in your sleep*]." So [*what, why, where*] I pray really isn't the big deal. The big deal is [*what, why, where*] I pray! When Jesus says, pray in your [*closet, pajamas, minivan*], he's making a point that I shouldn't be praying to get attention or [*squid, praise, money*] from other people.

Write a personal prayer to God here. Don't let anyone see it!

DARE THE TRUTH

24

Make it a Two-Way Street

Read: Matthew 6:14-15

WHAT JESUS SAID

Wow! Jesus was pretty clear on this one! He says you have to _____ people (Circle one word or phrase.)

PRAY   EAT CHEESE   run a marathon

forgive   give money   TOSS YOUR COOKIES

vote   hurry up   **serve**   ROLL OVER

How big of a deal is this to Jesus (according to these verses)? Add a needle to this meter.

Well, he wasn't kidding.

It's just a suggestion.   Whoa! Jesus was way serious!

If a movie were made about this dare, it could be called: (Pick one.)

WHAT JESUS MEANT

❑ Both or Nothing
❑ You Want? You Give!
❑ Pit Stains for Betty

❑ You Gotta Do It to Get It
❑ Two, Four, Give
❑ Other (Make one up.):

Why?

JESUS WAS TALKING TO ME

Give some (real) forgiveness advice to these people (No wimpy simple answers allowed!):

Penny really wants to forgive her friend Meg, but it's just not that simple. Meg blurted out Penny's biggest secret, just to get attention. And the worst part is: Meg doesn't even seem sorry. **What should Penny do?**

Derek loaned his skateboard to Sam, who didn't return it for a month. And when he finally returned it, it was all scraped up and tweaked. Sam said he was sorry—but it's not like he's offered to pay for the damage or anything. **What should Derek do?**

Write your name in each of the blanks. _____ totally ignores God all the time. _____ kinda wants to grow spiritually but chooses sin every single day. And _____ acts like God is a butler—always asking for stuff, but rarely hanging out with God or getting to know him better. **What should God do?**

DARE THE TRUTH

Be honest: we all have people in our lives who are hard to forgive. Name one:_____

Write a sentence or two about how and why you will forgive this person, and then put your signature and the date below:

_____   _____
              signed   date

Don't Tell

Read: Matthew 6:16–18

WHAT JESUS **SAID**

Jesus issued a whole series of dares along these lines: stuff that's for God (giving, praying) shouldn't be done to get attention for yourself. This is the last one. It's about: _____.

That word means:
- ❑ traveling really fast
- ❑ never eating—ever!
- ❑ giving something up for a period of time (usually food)

What's fasting all about?
- ❑ The discipline of giving something up (like food) for a day or two helps us focus on God.
- ❑ The discipline of giving something up (like food) for a day or two makes God notice us.
- ❑ The discipline of giving up food is a great weight-loss plan.

WHAT JESUS **MEANT**

If you're gonna bother fasting, why wouldn't Jesus be pleased with it no matter how you do it—what's with the "make sure you look funky fresh" stuff?

JESUS WAS TALKING TO ME

Okay, let's be honest: almost everyone reading this has never tried fasting. So taking on a dare to be sunny and fresh when you fast (as opposed to depressed and worn-out looking) might be jumping ahead a bit. Jesus...

❑ demands that you fast.

❑ said this to other people—people who already fast.

❑ assumes you're already fasting when he lays down this dare!

So, the first question is: are you willing to try fasting? (Circle one.)

No way! I could never fast!   I doubt it.   I'll consider it.   Yes, I will definitely try fasting.

Why?

And...what's the purpose fasting again? (Underline one or two.)

To focus on God and listen to God

To lose weight (No, please don't underline this one!)

To think about how much Jesus went through for us

To earn points with God

DARE THE TRUTH

As a young teen, it will be pretty tricky for you to pull off fasting for a day without telling your parents or anyone. But see if you can do it and only tell your parents (or whoever takes care of you). And don't make a big deal out of it. No whining or telling people, "Oh, I'm so hungry, 'cause I'm not eating today—for God!" Can you do it? Don't forget: whenever you're hungry, think of everything Jesus gave up for you.

❑ Yup, I'll give it a shot.   ❑ Uh...I'm not sure I'm ready for this.

Go Long

Read: Matthew 6:19–21

 WHAT JESUS **SAID**

What does it mean to invest in something?
- ❏ to put money into something
- ❏ to put a vest on
- ❏ to put any resource (money, time, beans) into something, hoping to get more back someday

Most people see investing as a money thing. What other kinds of things can you invest in?

Besides money, what can you invest?

What's it mean to invest in a relationship?

 WHAT JESUS **MEANT**

What's it mean to invest in serving others?

What's it mean to invest in God-stuff?

JESUS WAS TALKING TO ME

What things—good and not so good—do young teens invest in?
(Check all that apply.)

- ❑ popularity
- ❑ grades
- ❑ video game skills
- ❑ sports
- ❑ email and 'net surfing
- ❑ happiness
- ❑ collections (music, cards, etc.)

- ❑ beef jerky
- ❑ petunias
- ❑ cleanliness
- ❑ x-ray vision
- ❑ the autobahn
- ❑ sleep
- ❑ hobbies

- ❑ friendships
- ❑ nacho cheese Doritos
- ❑ lost languages
- ❑ WWF
- ❑ phone time
- ❑ fake dog poop
- ❑ other:

Now go back and circle one or two things that you invest a lot in.

Why do you invest in that (or those)?

Do your investments have eternal value, like Jesus talked about?

Yup   Kinda   Maybe   Nope

Which of these investments would have eternal value?

- ❑ prayer
- ❑ silence (listening to God)
- ❑ learning about God

- ❑ worship
- ❑ serving people
- ❑ other:

- ❑ reading the Bible
- ❑ showing God's love to people

Chose one of the investments from the last list. (Circle it.)
What will you do about that investment this week?

DARE THE TRUTH

Look Good

Read: Matthew 6:23

WHAT JESUS **SAID**

This dare is about: (Choose one.)
- ❏ poor eyesight (you need glasses)
- ❏ poor choices of things you look at (you need more wisdom)
- ❏ poor lighting (you need a brighter light bulb)
- ❏ poor pizza (you need more cheese and pepperoni)

Basically, Jesus says...
- ❏ "If you look at darkness, you can't see well."
- ❏ "If you don't take care of your eyes, you'll need to get glasses."
- ❏ "If you eat bad pizza, you'll spew bad stuff."
- ❏ "If you look at bad stuff, it will fill you up with bad stuff."

Sometimes people say, "Your eyes are windows to your soul." What do you think that means?

WHAT JESUS **MEANT**

How can looking at bad stuff have a bad influence on you?

Why does Jesus care what you look at?

JESUS WAS TALKING TO ME

Eye Doctors R Us
Write an eye prescription for these students (Make sure it's realistic—something you could imagine doing if you were them):

Jeremy loves movies. He watches them all the time, at theaters, on DVD—you name it. And his parents don't have any rules for him in this area, so he pretty much watches whatever he wants, including tons of R-rated movies.

Mike is a big time Internet geek. He spends hours every day surfing and chatting and building Web sites. And like a lot of guys, he sometimes struggles with spending time on porn sites.

Megan spends a lot of her babysitting money buying fashion magazines. She loves to look at all the cool clothes and think about wearing them. She fantasized about how guys respond to her if she looked like the girls in the magazines. And she loves to read the articles about sexy stuff.

DARE THE TRUTH

Write about your eye problem (not a real eye problem, silly, but something you like to look at, but know you shouldn't)

Write how you'll put this dare into practice this week and not look at something that can have a bad influence on you. Be specific!

Don't Bow To It

Read: Matthew 6:24

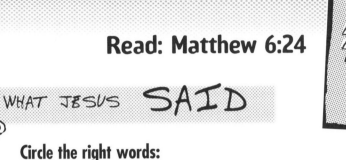

WHAT JESUS **SAID**

Circle the right words:

Jesus says we can't [*please, serve, campaign for*] Him and something else at the same time. It's in our nature to [*sin, love one, sell one*] and hate the other, or [*the other way around, need mental help, raise chickens*]. [*Turtles, Church, Money*] can be one of those "masters" or [*idols, wallets, fireside chats*]. It's impossible to have that be your major [*general, focus, in college*] and also serve [*tuna, yourself, God.*]

Write 5 cool things money can buy:

WHAT JESUS **MEANT**

1._____   4._____

2._____   5._____

3._____

Look back over that list. Cross out each one that can't compete with what God gives you.

On this scale draw a point to show how much of your focus God should get and how much of your focus money should get.

Money ●————————————————————————● God

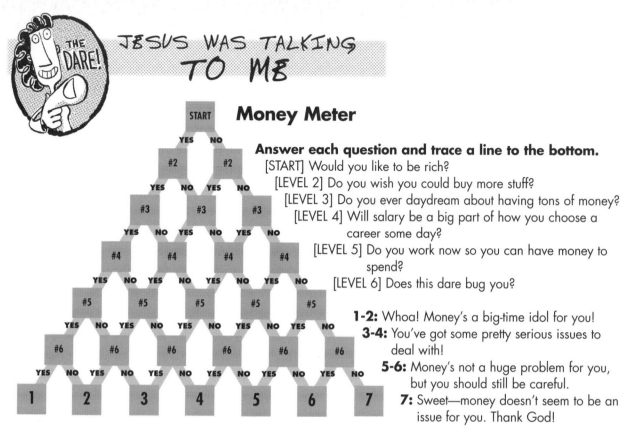

Money Meter

Answer each question and trace a line to the bottom.

[START] Would you like to be rich?

[LEVEL 2] Do you wish you could buy more stuff?

[LEVEL 3] Do you ever daydream about having tons of money?

[LEVEL 4] Will salary be a big part of how you choose a career some day?

[LEVEL 5] Do you work now so you can have money to spend?

[LEVEL 6] Does this dare bug you?

1-2: Whoa! Money's a big-time idol for you!

3-4: You've got some pretty serious issues to deal with!

5-6: Money's not a huge problem for you, but you should still be careful.

7: Sweet—money doesn't seem to be an issue for you. Thank God!

What's your response to this?

DARE THE TRUTH

This is a slippery one because it's about your heart-attitude. A "decision" here isn't really taking the dare. What can you do this week to make money less important in your life than God?

Will you do it?

Don't Waste Your Time

Read: Matthew 6:25–34

WHAT JESUS SAID

Draw a line to connect the things that go together (according to this passage):

each day •   • stow in barns
string cheese •   • dressed in splendor
birds •   • trouble of its own
lilies •   • peas and carrots

Worry can add _____ days to your life:
- ❑ 0
- ❑ 1
- ❑ 77
- ❑ 9,148
- ❑ who knows?

WHAT JESUS MEANT

Does God know who you are?   Yes   No

Does God care about you?   Yes No

Does God take care of lilies and birds?   Yes   No

Is God *able* to take care of you?   Yes   No

Are you worth more to God than lilies and birds?   Yes   No

Is it stupid to worry about stuff when God wants to take care of your needs?   Yes No

Did you answer "yes" to every one of these questions?   Yes   No, but I'll take this moment to change them.

JESUS WAS TALKING TO ME

Put stars next to the things teens your age worry about:

Are my grades good enough?

Do I look okay?

Am I popular enough?

Why can't cats and dogs get along?

Am I thin enough?

Do I stink?

Did Adam and Eve have belly buttons?

What am I going to do with my life?

Will I ever grow?

Will I ever have a date?

Will my parents split up?

Will I ever get super powers?

Will I get hurt at school?

Are my clothes cool enough?

Am I pretty enough?

Am I athletic enough?

What's the deal with France?

Will I get to go to heaven?

Will I ever stop growing?

Other:

Look back over the list, and circle the things you worry about the most.

Why do you worry about those things?

Do you think your worrying helps you or hurts you?

DARE THE TRUTH

Write a prayer here that turns your worries over to God and thanks him for taking care of you:

Look in the Mirror First

Read: Matthew 7:1-5

Hey dude! Um...not to be critical, but...

WHAT JESUS **SAID**

THE TRUTH

Okay, let's get a bit weird here. Draw a picture of the "you" described in this passage:

Other statements that would mean the same thing: (Check all that apply.)
- ❑ Take a minute to deal with the fact that you've lost all your fingernails, and then you can help your friend with her hangnail.
- ❑ Hey! Do something about your mouthful of green decaying teeth before offering someone a breath mint.
- ❑ First remove the pigeons roosting in your hair, and then you can point out your friend's bed head.

Which of these teens best summarizes what Jesus is talking about? (Check one)

WHAT JESUS **MEANT**

THE TRUTH

- ❑ Donna: "I think Jesus is trying to tell us that once we get our own act together and stuff, that we should tell our friends what they're doing wrong."
- ❑ Bobby: "Jesus was saying that it really bugs him when we judge other people. After all, we're all total sinners, right?"
- ❑ Virginia: "I'm not sure, but I think he was saying that it bugs him when we get stuff in our eyes, and that we're really idiots if we have big pieces of wood in there and stuff."

JESUS WAS TALKING TO ME

Answer these simple yes/no questions:

yes   no   Have you ever noticed someone's sin and thought less of him?

yes   no   Have you ever sinned yourself?

yes   no   Did you or do you deserve to be forgiven?

yes   no   Have you been forgiven?

yes   no   Since you've been forgiven for stuff that didn't deserve forgiveness, does it make sense that you can't really stand in judgment of others?

Why is this so difficult?

Why do you think so many Christians (and churches) spend so much energy judging people?

Whom have you been judging lately? (Write a name or two here.)

DARE THE TRUTH

What sin in your own life might you be ignoring—what's the "plank in your eye"? (Feel free to write in code if you're worried about someone seeing this.)

Pray for the person (or people) you've been judging. And ask God to forgive you for judging others.

By the way, Bobby was right (not Donna or Virginia).

Don't Sweat It!

Read: Matthew 7:7–11

WHAT JESUS **SAID**

Jesus wants to meet our:
❑ every wish and desire   ❑ needs   ❑ expectations

Jesus makes a comparison to a good father on earth with two questions. The obvious answer to those two questions is:

❑ of course!   ❑ because I said so!   ❑ of course not!

WHAT JESUS **MEANT**

What are some gifts you've received from your parents (or whoever you live with)?

What are some gifts you've received from God?

How good are the gifts?

parents' gifts

good ———————————— great ———————————— amazing!

God's gifts

good ———————————— great ———————————— amazing!

JESUS WAS TALKING TO ME

What are some of the needs young teens have? (Check all that apply.)

- ❑ love
- ❑ food
- ❑ lime Jell-O
- ❑ encouragement
- ❑ other:

- ❑ a place to sleep
- ❑ acceptance
- ❑ comfort
- ❑ gravy
- ❑ other:

- ❑ gummy bears
- ❑ a nice backpack
- ❑ a listener
- ❑ friendship

Now, look back over that list and circle the needs you have that God can meet.
Then put a star next to the ones that God can meet better than anyone else.

Unscramble these words:

DOG LIWI ETKA EARC FO LAL YM SNEED!

DARE THE TRUTH

Let God be God! Let him meet your needs. Look back at the list at the top of this page. Are any of those needs things that you've not been trusting God to meet? Are there any of those that you worry about or don't feel like they've been met? Either write about trusting God to meet a need or two, or write to ask God to meet a need or two you've struggled with (remember: "If your son asks for a fish, will you give him a snake?"). Write here:

Do It First

Read: Matthew 7:12

WHAT JESUS **SAID**

Basically, Jesus said...
...if you want someone to be nice to you, you should:

...if you want someone to listen to you, you should:

...if you want someone to smile at you, you should:

...if you want someone to be your friend, you should:

WHAT JESUS **MEANT**

Sometimes this verse is called:
- ❏ That Verse in Matthew
- ❏ The Purple Avenger
- ❏ The Golden Rule

This dare is best summed up by which sentence?
- ❏ Don't be a jerk.
- ❏ No shoes, no shirt, no service.
- ❏ Treat others how you want to be treated.

If a movie were made about this dare, which of these would be the best title?
- ❏ Can't We All Just Get Along?
- ❏ You First
- ❏ The Way to Live
- ❏ Other:

JESUS WAS TALKING TO ME

Okay, time for more honesty: this dare is so obvious, so simple, it would be silly to spend a bunch of time asking you questions like: "Should you be nice or mean?" So the issue here isn't helping you understand the dare—you're smart enough for that. But we need to spend a little space talking about why we don't live this out more often.

How do you treat lonely kids in your school?

How would you like to be treated if you were lonely?

What do you do for the old person in your neighborhood that has no one to visit him or her?

How would you like the neighborhood kids to treat you if you were an old person?

How do you treat the special ed students in your school?

How would you like to be treated if you were a special ed student?

DARE THE TRUTH

Think of a specific time this past week when you did NOT treat someone as you would like to have been treated. What happened?

How will you respond differently the next time the same thing happens?

Choose Your Destination

Read: Matthew 7:13-14

WHAT JESUS **SAID**

One gate is:
- ❏ wide
- ❏ wooden
- ❏ weird

and the other gate is:
- ❏ secret
- ❏ sunny
- ❏ small

One road is:
- ❏ bumpy
- ❏ broad
- ❏ bendy

and the other road is:
- ❏ narrow
- ❏ normal
- ❏ nonsense

Wide-way Blvd leads to:
- ❏ destiny
- ❏ desire
- ❏ destruction

Narrow Lane leads to:
- ❏ life
- ❏ loss
- ❏ loserville

Which of these best summarizes what Jesus meant?

WHAT JESUS **MEANT**

- ❏ It's almost impossible to live for God—so much so, that very few people are able to do it.

- ❏ You have a choice to live for yourself—which leads to death; or to live for God—which leads to life. Most people make the wrong choice.

- ❏ When you get your driver's license, you have to be very careful about those small and narrow streets—but they're lots of fun to drive on.

JESUS WAS TALKING TO ME

Why do you think the Jesus-way is so narrow? Why is the gate small?

Why is the other way wide and easy?

Do you think there are "exit ramps" that lead from the wide-way to the narrow-way and back? Do you choose the wide-way some days and the narrow-way others?   Yes   No
Write about that:

Claire's friends all met at the mall to go to a movie—but they hadn't decided ahead of time what they would see. When they checked out their options, all of Claire's friends wanted to see a new movie that was all about teenagers having sex and stuff. Claire knew it was a bad choice, but she didn't want to be the only one to sit out. So she went to the movie—she figured she could tell her friends afterward that they shouldn't have seen it.

Which way did Claire pick?   Wide   Narrow

Jonathan got a computer a couple years ago, and he loves to spend time online, looking at Web sites. But for the last six months, he's found that he's gotten totally hooked on looking on porn sites. It bugs him, and he knows it's wrong, but he can't seem to stop. But this week, Jonathan unplugged his computer, packed it back in the box, and asked his dad to store it away for 6 months. He told his dad he wanted to break some bad habits.

Which way did Jonathan pick?   Wide   Narrow

DARE THE TRUTH

In what areas of your life
do you struggle with choosing the road that leads to life?

What action do you need to take this week to take the Narrow Lane exit ramp off of Wide-way Boulevard?

Don't Be Foolish!

Read: Matthew 7:24–27

WHAT JESUS SAID

What Jesus said is similar to saying: (Check all that apply. Hint: They're not all correct.)

❑ Whoever puts what I say into practice is like a snowboarder with good bindings. She might fall, but it won't be because her bindings came loose. But whoever ignores what I say is like a snowboarder with lousy bindings. She'll be falling all over the place because her bindings won't hold.

❑ Whoever puts what I say into practice is like a baseball player wearing cleats. When he runs, he'll have great traction. But whoever ignores what I say is like a baseball player wearing sandals: he'll slip and fall around the corners.

❑ Whoever puts what I say into practice is like a perfectly made cheeseburger: plump, juicy, and dripping with real grade-A cheese. But whoever ignores what I say is like a bad cheeseburger: skanky, dripping with grease, and covered with fake and moldy cheese.

WHAT JESUS MEANT

The point of this dare is:
(Check one)
  ❑ worshipping Jesus
  ❑ knowing Jesus
  ❑ obeying Jesus   ❑ building houses with Jesus

The guy who built his house on the rock was: (Circle one.)

    Wise   Foolish

People who obey Jesus are: Wise   Foolish

The guy who built his house on the sand was: Wise   Foolish

People who hear, but don't obey Jesus, are: Wise   Foolish

JESUS WAS TALKING TO ME

Becca was reading her Bible the other day and saw where Jesus said not to ignore the poor. So today on her way home from school, while she was thinking about that, she walked past a homeless lady who asked Becca for some money. Becca had a dollar in her pocket. She walked to a nearby gas station and bought a bag of chips and brought them back to the lady.
Wise or Foolish? Why?

Shawn has heard lots of times that Jesus doesn't like gossip. But the crazy thing to Shawn is that everyone in his church—including the adults—seems to gossip all the time. Shawn figures he must not understand what Jesus was talking about.
Wise or Foolish? Why?

Jesus makes rules and boundaries for me...
❏ because he's a control freak who wants to mess with my life.
❏ because he loves me and wants me to have a great life.
❏ because he's religious, and religion is all about rules.

So, obeying Jesus is really...
❏ a complete and total drag.
❏ just what we have to do if we want to get to heaven.
❏ in my best interest. It will help me have a better life.

DARE THE TRUTH

Not obeying Jesus is like hitting yourself in the head with a rock: just plain foolish! In what area of your life have you ignored (at least once in a while) Jesus' teaching and desires for the way you should live?

What will you do (specifically) to be like the wise builder this week?

Go Big or Go Home

Read: Matthew 10:37-39

WHAT JESUS **SAID**

Which of these things is okay to love more than you love God?
(Check all that apply.)

- ❏ my mom
- ❏ my life
- ❏ cucumbers
- ❏ TV
- ❏ my personality
- ❏ prayer
- ❏ sleep

- ❏ my girlfriend/boyfriend
- ❏ my pet
- ❏ the Bible
- ❏ my computer
- ❏ my grandparents
- ❏ my friends
- ❏ um, nothing

- ❏ my bedroom
- ❏ my self-esteem
- ❏ my dad
- ❏ my youth leader
- ❏ nature
- ❏ my church

WHAT JESUS **MEANT**

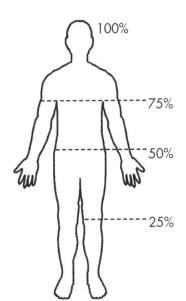

100%

75%

50%

25%

What percentage of you does Jesus want?
(Shade your answer.)

What does that mean?

47

JESUS WAS TALKING
TO ME

What are your options for choosing who will be in charge of your life? (Check all that apply.)

❏ you   ❏ your parents   ❏ your friends   ❏ God
❏ you and God together (some of each)   ❏ the government
❏ the winner of the Strongest Man in the World competition

What's the big problem with living for yourself and not for God?

Carli has decided she really isn't doing a very good job of managing her life. And she's pretty sure God would do a better job of it. She's even tried a little combo deal, where she gave God control of parts of her life (like the church parts and stuff), and she kept control of other parts (like the friends). But that didn't really work either. So she wants to try giving God complete control of her life. But she doesn't know how to go about actually doing this. **What would you tell her?**

DARE THE TRUTH

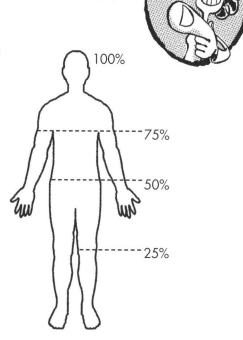

This dare is about giving God complete control of your life and trusting him totally. Where are you? How much of your life have you given over to God's control? C'mon, be honest. (Shade in your answer.)

What area of your life have you been holding back, that you'll give to God today?

100%

----75%

----50%

----25%

Lighten Your Load

Read: Matthew 11:28–30

WHAT JESUS SAID

Jesus wants to give you: (Check one)
❑ zits ❑ rest ❑ Bible-smarts ❑ a new car

To get this, we have to:
❑ work really hard ❑ sit up and beg
❑ be good ❑ go to him (Ooh, it's so complicated!)

WHAT JESUS MEANT

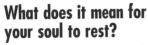

**What does it mean for
your soul to rest?**
❑ take a good long afternoon nap
❑ give your soul a break—allow yourself to stop being spiritual
for a little while
❑ give God everything we owe him
❑ have confidence that God is in control and that we can calm down
and be at peace

Why would you need this?

JESUS WAS TALKING TO ME

Provide the missing dialog for the characters in this short drama:

You: God, I'm tellin' ya, my life is way stressful right now.

God: Why don't you tell me about it?

You: Well, first there's this situation:_____

_____

_____

God: That does sound pretty stressful!

You: And that's not all.

God: _____

You: Are you sure you have time to listen to me?

God: _____

You: Okay, well, the other thing that's stressing me out is: _____

_____

_____

God: Well, I'd love to help you.

You: Can you make it all go away?

God: Yes, I could—but I'm not going to. You need some of this stuff. But what I *will* do is give you peace. I'll calm your soul.

You: What do I have to do?

God: Nothing! You've already done it by coming to me.

You: Ahhhhhhhhhhh.

In what areas of your life do you need to experience God's peace?

DARE THE TRUTH

Write a couple sentences asking God to give peace to your soul:

Join the Family

Read: Matthew 12:47–50

WHAT JESUS **SAID**

Identify the characters in this passage: (Check all that apply)

- ❏ Jesus
- ❏ Jesus' sisters
- ❏ Me
- ❏ Jesus' mother
- ❏ Jesus' pet Iguana, Hank
- ❏ the Disciples
- ❏ Jesus' brothers
- ❏ You
- ❏ Someone

Finish the sentence: I am Jesus' brother or sister when I...

WHAT JESUS **MEANT**

When we become God followers, God says we become:

- ❏ freaks
- ❏ his children
- ❏ hamsters
- ❏ heaven-bound!

And, since the J-man is God's Son, that means we are the _____ of Jesus:

- ❏ freaks
- ❏ children
- ❏ words
- ❏ brother or sister

Is this way cool?! (circle one)

 no

JESUS WAS TALKING TO ME

I suppose it's only fair to say Jesus' words go a bit further than saying, "Hey, congrats—you're my bro or sis!" 'Cause there's also a dare in there (Ooh, that rhymes!). **The dare is:** (Circle a letter.)

    a. If ya wanna be my bro or sis, ya gotta pay dues.
    b. If ya wanna be my bro or sis, ya gotta do family chores.
    c. If ya wanna be my bro or sis, ya gotta obey our dad.

Put stars next to Jesus' most likely response to each student:

Sherry told the truth even when she knew it would get her in trouble.
    J sez: "Yo, you are my sis!"
    J sez: "Who are you?"

Wade serves in the kid's class at church, although his buddies make fun of him for it.
    J sez: "Brudda WADE!"
    J sez: "Hi, have we met?"

Steve constantly pummels his little sister Gwen.
    J sez: "Hey, Stevie—brutha!"
    J sez: "Um, Steve who?"

DARE THE TRUTH

**You know it. I know it. We all know the difference between right and wrong.
So stop using that "but I didn't know" whiney excuse! In what area(s) of your life are you struggling with obeying God?**

What do you need to do about this?

Forget Yourself, Follow Jesus

Read: Matthew 16:24-27

WHAT JESUS **SAID**

There seems to be one good choice with two parts. It is: (Check one)
- ❏ follow Jesus and try to balance that with your own needs
- ❏ follow Jesus and leave the other stuff behind
- ❏ hold onto the world and hold onto Jesus
- ❏ eat the salami and the cheese

If you wanna save your life, you gotta _____

But if you lose your life for Jesus, you'll _____

The best summary of this dare is:

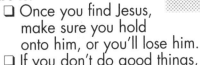

WHAT JESUS **MEANT**

- ❏ Once you find Jesus, make sure you hold onto him, or you'll lose him.
- ❏ If you don't do good things, Jesus will not accept you when he returns.
- ❏ Follow hard after Jesus, and don't get distracted by other things.
- ❏ Make sure you use cheese *and* salami—either by itself is just not as good.

When Jesus says he'll reward us "according to what we've done" when he returns, he doesn't mean that we should do good stuff to earn points with him. The "what we've done" refers to:
- ❏ whether or not we've chosen to follow him
- ❏ if the good stuff we've done weighs more than the bad stuff we've done
- ❏ if we properly combined the cheese and salami

JESUS WAS TALKING TO ME

Dani is a great gymnast. She read this verse and decided it means she has to give up her dream of being a gymnast and quit. What would you say to her?

Pablo really wants to live for Jesus. His understanding of this dare is that he needs to make sure nothing in his life is more important than Jesus. What would you say to him?

Jessie is struggling: she became a Jesus-follower this past summer at camp, and she wants to live for God. But she really likes partying and doing a bunch of stuff her youth worker always tells her she shouldn't. She's thinking that everything seems to be going just fine as it is. What would you say to her?

What will it mean for you to "give up your life to find it"? Are there things you need to give up? Write about that.

DARE THE TRUTH

Be a Child

Read: Matthew 18:1-5

WHAT JESUS SAID

This dare says:

❑ If you act really immature and throw childish hissy fits, Jesus will smile on you.

❑ If you have the complete trust and faith that children have, you'll have the kind of faith God wants for you.

❑ If you find a time machine and physically become a child again, you will have achieved the highest possible spiritual goal.

What is it about children that Jesus holds up as an example for us?
(Check all that apply.)

WHAT JESUS MEANT

❑ their lack of doubts
❑ their innocence
❑ their belief (how easily they believe)

❑ their purity
❑ their temper tantrums
❑ the fact that they eat glue and crayons

So many things in God's kingdom are upside-down from our world's values. Our world

values _____, but Jesus values _____.
            (a)   (b)

a: (Choose one.)
strength and power
money and wealth
canned peaches

b: (Choose one.)
fresh peaches
good behavior
purity

JESUS WAS TALKING TO ME

What does it mean to have a pure faith?

Rate these kids from "most childlike faith" (1) to "least childlike faith" (4):

___ Jack acts like a little child all the time. He whines and demands his way. He's selfish and thinks the world revolves around him.

___ Simone struggles with all kinds of deep questions about her faith. This is good 'cause she wants to find the truth. But it also causes her to doubt God all the time.

___ Natasha's very smart, but she's decided it makes no sense to waste her time making God prove himself to her. She's choosing to trust that God knows what he's doing.

___ Aaron really loves Jesus. Sure, life isn't always easy. But Aaron's biggest passion in life is to serve God and worship him.

How childlike (and pure) is your faith? Draw an outline of a person here—a little kid or a teen or an adult—to represent what your faith looks like. Remember, there's a difference between "childish" and "childlike"!

DARE THE TRUTH

Spend a few minutes praying, asking God to help you have a more childlike faith. Pray through these ideas:

❏ God, help my faith be more pure. Help me to focus on you.

❏ God, I don't want to doubt you—I want to believe. Help me believe.

❏ God, help me to give up more control to you. Help me be less interested in controlling my life.

❏ God, I love you, and I want to love you more. Help me grow in my love for you.

❏ God, help me to speak about you to others without embarrassment.

❏ God, help me to jump into your arms with complete trust!

Don't Mess With Little Ones

Read: Matthew 26:10-9

WHAT JESUS SAID

According to this verse, God really cares about...
❑ truth   ❑ church   ❑ kids   ❑ burritos

If you mess with (the answer to the first question), you'd be better off...
❑ riding carnival rides forever (hurl!).   ❑ on your knees praying constantly.
❑ swimming with the fishies, permanently.   ❑ as the person who empties porta-potties.

WHAT JESUS MEANT

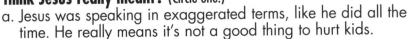

This sounds way harsh, doesn't it? Which of these do you think Jesus really meant? (Circle one.)

    a. Jesus was speaking in exaggerated terms, like he did all the time. He really means it's not a good thing to hurt kids.

    b. Jesus really meant what he said—he cares a lot about little kids and has no patience for people who hurt them.

    c. Who knows what Jesus meant?

What are different ways that people hurt kids? (List at least five.)

JESUS WAS TALKING TO ME

What ways do young teens hurt little kids? (Check all that apply.)
- ❏ bully them around
- ❏ hurt their feelings
- ❏ feed them dog biscuits
- ❏ hurt them physically
- ❏ say "no" to them
- ❏ lead them into sin
- ❏ ignore them
- ❏ steal their Legos
- ❏ other:

If Jesus makes such a big deal out of not hurting little kids, he probably wants you to do just the opposite, which is: (Circle all the words that apply.)

help them   launch them   bug them   encourage them

love them   tax the   protect them   other:

How can young teens do this? (Write at least 10 ideas.)

1.   6.

2.   7.

3.   8.

4.   9.

5.   10.

What little kid can you build up this week? (If you have a little bro or sis, start there!) Write a name here:

DARE THE TRUTH

_____

How will you do this?

Get Along!

Read: Matthew 18:15–35

WHAT JESUS **SAID**

If you had only read verses 15-17, you'd think this dare was about:
- ❏ tuna salad and its important role in world history
- ❏ the difference between loving God and loving yourself
- ❏ how to confront someone who's hurt you

If you had only read verses 19-20, you'd think this dare was about:
- ❏ obeying your parents
- ❏ praying with friends
- ❏ breeding emus for fun and profit

If you had only read verses 21-35, you'd think this dare was about:
- ❏ forgiving people who hurt you
- ❏ breaking the silence about the pain of those with excess snot
- ❏ reading your Bible regularly

WHAT JESUS **MEANT**

But, if you read the whole thing together (which, of course, being the amazing teen you are, you did), you have to come to the conclusion that this super-dare is about:
- ❏ the importance of going to church and being part of a Christian community
- ❏ how much God cares about his children getting along with each other
- ❏ how annoying it is that CDs cost less to make than cassette tapes, but we have to pay so much more for them!

Relate-o-meter

START

YES   NO
#2   #2

YES   NO   YES   NO
#3   #3   #3

YES NO YES NO YES NO
#4   #4   #4   #4

YES NO YES NO YES NO YES NO
#5   #5   #5   #5   #5

YES NO YES NO YES NO YES NO YES NO
#6   #6   #6   #6   #6   #6

YES NO YES NO YES NO YES NO YES NO YES NO
1   2   3   4   5   6   7

Answer each question and trace a line to the bottom. (Be honest!)

[START] Are you sometimes grumpy and hard to get along with?

[LEVEL 1] Are you an independent person who doesn't like to rely on others for help?

[LEVEL 2] Do you have people in your life right now that you haven't forgiven?

[LEVEL 3] Are you stingy with people (not generous)?

[LEVEL 4] Do you like to get revenge?

[LEVEL 5] Do you hold grudges?

[LEVEL 6] Do you ever gossip?

1 = Sweet: you're doing great at relationships! (Don't get a big head, now!)

2-3 = Be careful: think about whether you have areas where you need to grow in how you treat other people.

4-5 = Uh-oh: you've got some serious business to do with God in this area of your life.

6-7 = Trouble!: get busy, 'cause you've got a *lot* of growing to do in this area of your life!

DARE THE TRUTH

God made all of us, and he wants us to get along with each other. Because he loves us, he designed us to have good relationships with each other. As you worked through this lesson, what areas or relationships stood out to you as something you need to grow in?

What real step of action will you take this week? (Make sure this action step feels like a dare!)

Do It Again and Again

Read: Matthew 26:10–9

WHAT JESUS SAID

Jesus said:

❑ "I've got a suggestion for you: stop being a bonehead. Shape up, buster, or you're going to be in lots of trouble, if you know what I mean."

❑ "Here's the deal: I forgave you, right? And the stuff I forgave you for is a much bigger deal than how you've been wronged. So, you better be forgiving others!"

❑ "Thank you, flight attendant; but I'd greatly prefer the grilled chicken salad. Please take back this squid-burger."

WHAT JESUS MEANT

Jesus tells a great little story in this passage to illustrate this dare.

Rewrite the story in a modern setting with teens as characters:

JESUS WAS TALKING TO ME

It makes sense, doesn't it, that forgiveness would be such a big deal to Jesus? I mean, after all, he gave up his life to give you and me forgiveness we didn't deserve. Give these kids some forgiveness advice: but don't wimp out and just write, "Forgive her" as your answer! Sometimes forgiving people is hard work, and specific ideas can help!

For 3 years, Janelle's best friend has been Corin. But in the last few weeks, Corin has totally turned her back on Janelle. Corin started hanging out with a much more popular group of kids at school. She ignores Janelle and even treats her poorly in front of her "new" friends. Should Janelle forgive Corin? If so, how?

Julius has had a ton of anger toward his dad for 8 years, ever since Julius' dad left him and his mom when Julius was 6. His dad showed up again this year, and he's trying to be "dad" again—and Julius just isn't sure he wants anything to do with the guy. Should Julius forgive his dad? If so, how?

DARE THE TRUTH

Pick the one person in your life right now that is hardest for you to forgive. Write a name or initials here: _____
Maybe you can get to total forgiveness of this person this week, or maybe you just need to take a first action step. What will you do? (Choose one or more, or write your own action step.)

❏ Tell two people you trust about this issue and that you want to forgive this person. Ask these people to hold you accountable and to ask you about it from time to time.
❏ Call the person you have an issue with and schedule a time to meet and talk about the issue. Go into this with *no* intent to convince them they did anything wrong—just with a desire to forgive.
❏ Write a couple notes: one to God, asking him to help you forgive this person; and one to the person, expressing your desire to forgive them. You don't have to give the letter to them—just write it.
❏ other:

Give Your Whole Heart

Read: Matthew 22:34-38

WHAT JESUS **SAID**

This dare says to love God with all your: (Check all that apply.)
❑ heart   ❑ spleen   ❑ soul   ❑ mind   ❑ money   ❑ cabbage

He also said that this is more important than: (Check one)
❑ getting good grades   ❑ finishing everything on your plate
❑ anything else   ❑ memorizing Bible verses

Rewrite verses 37 and 38 here, in your own words:

WHAT JESUS **MEANT**

Why is this such a big deal to Jesus? (Don't just say, "'Cause he wants us to love him.")

JESUS WAS TALKING TO ME

How can you show God that you love him? (Check all that apply)

- ❑ use the gifts and abilities he's given you
- ❑ act religious
- ❑ worship him
- ❑ hold up John 3:16 signs at sporting events
- ❑ say "Praise God" all the time
- ❑ stick a fish on your car
- ❑ watch religious TV
- ❑ love other people (They're God's creation!)
- ❑ other:

- ❑ obey him
- ❑ obey your parents
- ❑ talk to him
- ❑ learn more about him
- ❑ read the Bible
- ❑ give money to him
- ❑ volunteer in your church
- ❑ listen to church leaders
- ❑ other:

Go back over that list and put stars next to the top three ways to love God.

One more time, look over that list and underline the ways you currently show God you love him. Only underline it if that method is something you do all the time (not just once in a while).

What difference do you think it will make in your life if you grow in your love for God?

DARE THE TRUTH

Look over the list at the top of this page (Yes, again—stop complaining!). Choose one way to show love to God that you would like to grow in. Circle that one.

What specific action will you take this week to grow in that area?

Love 'em Good

Read: Matthew 22:39

WHAT JESUS **SAID**

This dare is pretty stinkin' simple to understand (if not to carry out). Just as Jesus says, the dare is: love others like...
❏ you mean it   ❏ your mamma loves you
❏ you love yourself   ❏ God loves you

WHAT JESUS **MEANT**

This one's a bit slippery since you might not think you love yourself very much ("If I don't love myself, does that mean I can treat other people like dirt?"). **But here's the story, self-lover...**(Circle your answer.)

True   False   I like to make decisions that please me.

True   False   When given a few choices, I choose the option that is best for me (assuming it's not illegal or immoral).

True   False   In doing this, I'm showing that I love myself (even if I don't always like myself).

True   False   The answer to all these questions is probably "true" for everybody.

True   False   Anyone who doesn't circle "true" for all of these either doesn't understand the questions or isn't telling the truth.

True   False   So, if we all really do love ourselves (at least by making choices that are best for us), then we should love others by making choices that are best for them too.

True   False   This makes sense to me.

JESUS WAS TALKING TO ME

Other-Lovers
Rate these teens on how well they're carrying out this dare (1 to 5, 5 being best)

____ Carrie helps set up the sound system every Sunday morning—and she has to be at church at 7 a.m. to get started. She doesn't ever want to be on the platform, but this gives her a way to help people worship.

____ Justin loves people, especially girls. He's constantly giving people hugs and saying, "love ya" and stuff like that.

____ Maddie knows this girl in her science class is lonely, 'cause she's brand-new to Maddie's school. Maddie decides the best thing for this girl would be if Maddie asked to be her science project partner.

____ Ricky knows he won the wrestling match, but the ref didn't call it that way. Ricky decides that the best choice is to let it go and congratulate his opponent.

____ Bethany's little brother David is always bugging her. Today he asked her to kick a soccer ball around the backyard. Bethany *really* doesn't want to, but she decided to have a good attitude and kick the ball with him for a little while.

List a bunch of ways you can show love to other people:

Name someone that would be a challenge for you to show some love to:

DARE THE TRUTH

How could you love that person like yourself this week?

Will you do it? Yes No Maybe

Start at the Back

Read: Matthew 23:12

WHAT JESUS **SAID**

Circle the correct words or phrases in this paragraph:

If you spend a lot of time [*frying your bacon, strutting your stuff, walking your goose*], then you'll end up [*the lowest of the low, the king of the world, the cat's meow*]. But if you approach life with [*guns ablazin', a healthy self-esteem, a humble attitude*], then God will [*lift you up, give you zits, let you into heaven*].

Jesus doesn't want you to: (Check all that are NOT what Jesus was saying.)

WHAT JESUS **MEANT**

❑ think you're a total dirtbag
❑ eat your toenails

❑ be humble
❑ hate yourself

What kinds of things does a person full of puffed-up pride do?

What kinds of things does a person full of humility do?

JESUS WAS TALKING TO ME

It's a bit backward to say you're great at humility ("I'm the most humble person I know!"). But try to be honest here. Rate yourself on this humility meter (Add a needle to show your humility level.)

I've got a lot of pride, not much humility.

I struggle with being humble, but I'm doing okay.

I have NO humility: I'm a puffed-up pride freak.

No one is more humble than the great me!

What's the difference between healthy pride ("I'm proud to be a part of this team." "I'm very excited that my poem won the competition.") and the kind of destructive pride Jesus is talking about?

DARE THE TRUTH

A humble person knows that the good stuff in her life (accomplishments, abilities) is there because of God. That's what gives her humility. In what area(s) of your life have you been taking credit for honor that really belongs to God?

Write a prayer here, giving God credit for that success in your life:

Go Get 'Em

Read: Matthew 28:18-20

WHAT JESUS **SAID**

THE TRUTH

Which of the following are key action words from this dare? (Circle all that apply.)

run   go   drink

barf   make   toss   baptize

prepare   hypnotize   teach

screech   faint

What's the result if you carry out this dare?
- ❑ many, many more church potluck suppers
- ❑ lots of people saying, "praise-a-luia"
- ❑ baptized, God-obeying disciples of Jesus
- ❑ riding off into the sunset

WHAT JESUS **MEANT**

THE TRUTH

The big word for this dare is:
- ❑ procrastination
- ❑ premillennialism
- ❑ evangelism
- ❑ homiletics

Which of these verses best summarizes the dare? (Ha! Yup, you've got to look them up!)
- ❑ Acts 20:9
- ❑ 1 Samuel 24:3
- ❑ 1 Peter 3:15

JESUS WAS TALKING TO ME

This is the dare of all dares! Get out there: share your faith in Jesus Christ! Since it's not likely you'll travel to the four corners of the world this year, what are some ways you can "make disciples of all nations"? (Check all that apply.)

- ❏ I can open up my mouth and share the hope I have in Jesus Christ with a friend at school.
- ❏ I can slip scripture verses into the fortune cookies at my local Chinese restaurant.
- ❏ I can invite a friend to a youth group activity where she will hear Jesus' story.
- ❏ I can give money to support missionaries from my church.
- ❏ I can run through busy intersections holding a John 3:16 sign.
- ❏ I can spend time praying for friends that don't know Jesus.
- ❏ I can go on a short-term missions trip and tell people about Jesus.
- ❏ I can take control of my school announcement system and read the book of Leviticus to my fellow students.
- ❏ Other:

Why is telling people about Jesus so difficult for most of us? Why is it difficult for you?

Look back at the list at the top of this page. Put stars next to TWO ideas you'll try this week. Write here how you'll go about doing them:

DARE THE TRUTH

Believe It

Read: Mark 11:23-24

WHAT JESUS SAID

Jesus wants us to have lots and lots of:
❑ mustard ❑ money ❑ Bibles ❑ faith

And if we do have lots of that stuff, we can:
❑ have really good hot-dogs ❑ see our prayers get answered
❑ make a big difference in the world ❑ run a 3-minute mile

Which of these paragraphs best summarizes what Jesus meant? (Circle one.)

WHAT JESUS MEANT

If you have a lot of faith, mountains will be flyin' all over the place. You can do anything. You can pray, "I want four red Ferrari's in my driveway right now." And—poof!—they'll instantly appear (if you have faith). You can pray, "I want to be king of the world." And, if you have faith, you'll be wearing a crown in no time flat!

If you have a lot of faith, amazing things can happen. God wants you to pray with an attitude of faith, believing that what you ask for will really happen. That doesn't mean every time you ask for a thousand CDs, and really believe it, that—poof!—they'll appear on your shelf. But it does mean that God wants us to believe that he can do what we ask him to do.

If you have a lot of faith, everything will be perfect forever. You'll never get sick again. No one you love will ever die. There will be peace all over the world all the time. Evil will go away. Everyone will be nice to you all the time. You'll be perfectly successful and never experience pain again in your entire life. All if you just have a little more faith.

JESUS WAS TALKING TO ME

Which of these is a prayer of faith? (Check all that are.)

❑ God, I'm having a hard time liking my new step-dad. But I know you want the best for me; and I know you want the best for my mom. So I'm choosing to trust you, God, that you'll take care of us, and you'll help me to like him.

❑ God, I'm sick of those meanies in my math class. Make 'em all go away forever.

❑ God, I'm going to invite Sharon to youth group tonight. And I'm totally freaked about it. I really need you to give me courage, okay?

❑ God, can I have a million dollars?

❑ God, I suppose you could make my life better, but I don't think you even notice me. So...if you're there, do something.

❑ I know you know about my secret sin, God. I can't seem to stop. But I know you can help me. So I'm asking—obviously I can't do it without you.

Write about a time you prayed for something and it happened:

Write a prayer of faith. C'mon—get bold and ask God to meet some needs, and exercise real faith that he will!

DARE THE TRUTH

Give Big

Read: Luke 6:38

WHAT JESUS **SAID**

This dare is about:
- ❑ gravy
- ❑ giving
- ❑ God
- ❑ gallstones

Give little, get blessed _____.

Give more, get blessed _____.

Give a lot, get blessed _____.

WHAT JESUS **MEANT**

Normally, God doesn't like it when we "test" him. But this is one place in the Bible where Jesus clearly says, "C'mon, I dare you—try me out, and I'll show you!"
What are the different ways God might bless you in return for your giving? (Check all that might be true.)

- ❑ happiness
- ❑ cheese puffs
- ❑ stuff (money, et cetera)
- ❑ relationships
- ❑ more of God's presence
- ❑ contentment

- ❑ peace
- ❑ joy
- ❑ earwax
- ❑ pain and suffering
- ❑ healing
- ❑ other:

JESUS WAS TALKING TO ME

Which of the following are things teens can give that fit with this dare?

(Check all that apply.)

- ❑ rubber chickens
- ❑ service
- ❑ lint
- ❑ love
- ❑ attention
- ❑ dirty looks
- ❑ talents
- ❑ money
- ❑ hairballs
- ❑ gifts
- ❑ split pea soup
- ❑ presence
- ❑ time
- ❑ Spam
- ❑ encouragement
- ❑ other:

Look back over that list. Underline the kinds of giving you are regularly involved in. Then cross out the ones that you don't do very often.

Why is it so hard to give without expecting something in return, like a payback?

Look at the list at the top of this page once more. Put a star next to one or two ways that you would like to accept as a dare this week. Write that (or those) here:

DARE THE TRUTH

Now come up with a specific plan for carrying that out:

Fear Correctly

Read: Luke 12:4–5

WHAT JESUS **SAID**

There ain't no reason to fear:
❑ pasta ❑ people ❑ purple ❑ plasma

But there's plenty o' reasons to fear:
❑ goofballs ❑ gophers ❑ greed ❑ God

WHAT JESUS **MEANT**

If you played one-on-one basketball with the best basketball player in the world, what would your attitude be while playing?

If you wrestled with an extremely large grizzly bear that was tame, how would you feel during the match (every time you saw those teeth, or when one of those claws whizzed past your face)?

Fearing God is about being aware of his potential. It's great that we spend a lot of time talking about God as our friend or our daddy. But it's important to remember whom we're talking about: the creator of the universe who holds the keys to heaven and hell and can create or destroy by saying a word. Fearing God is about respect.

JESUS WAS TALKING TO ME

Put a needle on these meters to rate how you treat God:

I sometimes think of God this way

I don't think of God this way

I think of God this way all the time

"God is my friend"

I sometimes think of God this way

I don't think of God this way

I think of God this way all the time

"God is to be feared"

Now go back to those meters; and with a different needle design, or different color pen, rate where you think you *should* be on each of them.

Do you have any thoughts about the difference between "fearing God" and "being afraid of God"? (There is a difference!) Write those thoughts here:

DARE THE TRUTH

Take the dare: Brainstorm (sometime this week) ten reasons God should be feared. And find a few verses in the Bible that talk about fearing God (There are TONS of them!).

If you'll take this dare, sign here:

_____

Then come back and check this box once you've competed the dare ❑

Don't Be Greedy

Read: Luke 12:15

WHAT JESUS **SAID**

Which of these is the best title for this dare?
- ❑ Gotta Get It
- ❑ I Want What You've Got
- ❑ You Aren't Your Stuff
- ❑ He Who Dies with the Most Toys Wins

This dare is different from a lot of others 'cause it doesn't just say, "Do this!" Instead, Jesus says...
- ❑ "Listen to your mother!"
- ❑ "Just say no!"
- ❑ "Don't do this!"
- ❑ "Be careful!"

If Jesus is warning us like that, it must mean that greed is:

WHAT JESUS **MEANT**

- ❑ easy to get sucked into
- ❑ a ball o' fun
- ❑ a ticket to hell
- ❑ best with Parmesan cheese

Define greed:

How is greed like a trap?

JESUS WAS TALKING TO ME

Which teen shows the most greed?

(Rank from most greedy [1] to least greedy [3])

___ Charise is so excited! Some guy at church was cleaning out his CD collection, and he gave her 25 awesome CDs. Her friend Carmen is standing by her when the guy gives the CDs to Charise. Charise tells Carmen, "I guess you can have one."

___ Conner enjoys nothing more than spending time with his best friend David. And when a new kid starts coming to the youth group, and David suggests they ask him to join them, Conner says, "Dude! We can't break up our friendship by including someone else!"

___ Brittney baby-sits for some rich people, and she gets paid tons of money. But when she heard her pastor challenging people to give ten percent of what they earn to God, she thought to herself, "But that's *my* money—I earned it myself."

Greedometers– How greedy are you? (Be honest!)

About money...

not at all   way greedy!

About friends...

not at all   way greedy!

About "your stuff"...

not at all   way greedy!

About time...

not at all   way greedy!

Write about a recent time when you were greedy:

DARE THE TRUTH

What can you do, this week, to make that right?

Come back and check here ❏ when you've done it.

Prove It

Read: Luke 16:10–12

WHAT JESUS **SAID**

Jesus wants to trust you with...(Circle the correct answers)

First, show you can be trusted with…	LITTLE THINGS	BIG THINGS
Really, if you can't be trusted with…	LITTLE THINGS	BIG THINGS
Then how can you be trusted with…	LITTLE THINGS	BIG THINGS
But if you prove that you can be trusted with…	LITTLE THINGS	BIG THINGS
Then you can bet you'll be trusted with…	LITTLE THINGS	BIG THINGS

Which of these teens understands this dare?

WHAT JESUS **MEANT**

- ❏ Karla has natural ability as a flute player. But every time she plays in front of people, she gets full of pride.

- ❏ Jacob has a job working for his uncle, cleaning up a gas station. He doesn't really like it very much, but he tries to do a great job, 'cause he knows it will teach him good stuff about work.

- ❏ Jing May is part of a group of kids who clean up parks on weekends. None of the other teens are Jesus followers, but Jing May does it because she believes it's what God wants her to do to take care of the earth.

JESUS WAS TALKING TO ME

What kinds of things would God entrust to a teen? (Check all that apply.)

- ❑ money
- ❑ facial hair
- ❑ mud
- ❑ recognition
- ❑ chances to love others
- ❑ other:

- ❑ jobs
- ❑ talents
- ❑ family
- ❑ friendships

- ❑ leadership
- ❑ responsibilities
- ❑ success
- ❑ stuff
- ❑ opportunities to talk about Jesus
- ❑ other:

- ❑ meatloaf
- ❑ abilities
- ❑ the earth
- ❑ Styrofoam peanuts

Make sure you add two more things in those spaces that say "other."

Write about something you've been really trustworthy with:

Write about something you haven't been very trustworthy with:

DARE THE TRUTH

Choose one item from the list at the top of this page, and write a plan for being trustworthy with it this week:

Do What You Have to Do

Read: Luke 17:7–10

WHAT JESUS **SAID**

Servants in the field, when brought dinner by another servant, don't say:
- ❏ "I'm sure you could find me something better to eat!"
- ❏ "Oh no, you shouldn't bring me food—you should let me serve you!"

They say:
- ❏ "Oh good, my food's here."
- ❏ "What can I do to serve *you*, my good friend and fellow servant?"

In the same way, when we do what God asks us to do, we should say:
- ❏ "Hey, God—did you notice what I did? Can you give me something cool for doing it?"
- ❏ "There—I did what I was supposed to do."

WHAT JESUS **MEANT**

Rank these titles for this dare from best (1) to worst (5):
- ___ 'Tis My Duty
- ___ I'm a Maggot; I'm a Dirtball
- ___ I Did What I Did 'Cause That's What I Do
- ___ What Have You Done for Me Lately?
- ___ I Did It My Way

This has something to say about:
- ❏ the benefits of being God's children
- ❏ our reason for doing good things
- ❏ cinnamon sugar toast
- ❏ chugga-lugging root beer

JESUS WAS TALKING TO ME

☐ Teri: "God? I want you to know something. I mean, I know you already know everything; but I want to point this out to you in case you were too busy to notice. I was nice to my snotty little brother this morning. Now, I'm hoping that in return for this good deed, you can get him to leave me along for a week or two. What do you say?"

☐ Philip: "Hey God. It's very cool to live for you. I mean, I don't always *like* it—the obeying stuff and all—but I know your plans for me are good. So I'll do whatever you ask me to do—to the best of my understanding. I'm sure I'll mess up sometimes. But I want you to know that my goal is to do what you ask me to do."

☐ Shonda: "This afternoon, God, the lady at the store gave me too much money back, you know? And it was hard to point it out to her—not just 'cause I wanted the money, but because I knew my friends would laugh at me, which they did. Anyhow, I'm not mentioning this because I want anything from you. Just the opposite: I wanted to thank you for giving me the courage to do what's right."

☐ James: "I don't get it, God. I've been trying to do good stuff: I wore a Jesus T-shirt; I asked a friend to go to a youth group party; I did my chores last week without complaining. But c'mon, God—how come you haven't answered that prayer of mine for a new motorcycle? I scratched your back—it's time for you to scratch mine!"

List at least 6 things that are our duty if we choose to follow God. In other words, what are some of the things we should see as "just part of being a servant of the king"?

DARE THE TRUTH

Choose one or two of the things you just listed that you struggle with. Circle them. Now write a plan here for what you can do about them this week:

Walk Away

Read: Luke 18:29–30

WHAT JESUS **SAID**

If you took this dare literally (just what it says), you would
(Check all that apply)

- ❏ say bye-bye to your wifey
- ❏ say *adios* to your brothers
- ❏ checkout on your parents!
- ❏ leave those kids behind

- ❏ run around the block
- ❏ three words: move, move, move
- ❏ paddle like there's no tomorrow
- ❏ bolt from house

Which of these fake movie plotlines best summarizes this dare?

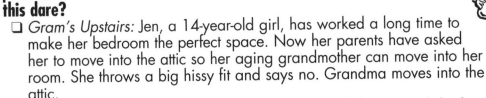

WHAT JESUS **MEANT**

- ❏ *Gram's Upstairs:* Jen, a 14-year-old girl, has worked a long time to make her bedroom the perfect space. Now her parents have asked her to move into the attic so her aging grandmother can move into her room. She throws a big hissy fit and says no. Grandma moves into the attic.
- ❏ *Return to Animals:* A young boy had a barnyard full of animals he loved. But his uncle in another land asked him to come take care of him in his old age. The boy chose to leave his animals and take care of his uncle. To his great surprise, he found that his uncle had four times as many animals for him to love and take care of.
- ❏ *The Car-Rotty Kid:* A poor kid from the wrong part of town learns karate from a weird old guy and becomes the state champion. But in the end, the old guy's car falls apart.

Why did you choose that plotline? What does it have to do with this dare?

JESUS WAS TALKING
TO ME

Give advice to this teen, to help her take this dare:

Stacy runs track for her school, and she's really good at it. But she's got a major conflict on her hands. She made a commitment to help with her church's Vacation Bible School—a program for little kids, before she found out it's the same week as a track camp her coach wants her to attend.

What should Stacy do? What would you do—really—if you were in Stacy's place?

What might happen if she makes that choice?

The bottom line here is:
- ❑ **Discipline:** how hard are you willing to work for God?
- ❑ **Obedience:** what are you willing to give up in order to follow God?
- ❑ **Nasal cleanliness:** how spiffy are you willing to keep your nose holes?

Can you think of anything you've been holding on to that you know you need to give up to really follow God? Write about that here:

DARE THE TRUTH

What can you do about it this week?

Give 'Til It Hurts

Read: Luke 21:2-4

ouch.

ouch!

WHAT JESUS SAID

Circle the correct words in this paragraph:

Jesus and his buddies were standing outside [*Pizza Hut, the temple, the town hall*], and they saw [*a flamingo, a priest, a widow*] put [*two small coins, a load of banana bread, a comment card*] into [*the fountain, a video game, the collection box*]. Jesus pointed out that [*she needed to comb her hair, it was sad that her husband had died, her giving was a really big deal*].

WHAT JESUS MEANT

In Jesus' time, widows (women whose husbands died) had:
- ❑ very few ways to find a new husband
- ❑ tons of money from the government
- ❑ very few ways to earn money and were usually very poor
- ❑ to wear big Ws on their clothes, so people would know they're widows

The widow giving two small coins was the most like: (Check two)
- ❑ one homeless person giving his shoes to another homeless person
- ❑ a multi-millionaire giving a $100,000 to his church
- ❑ a teenager giving a compliment to someone who's not nice to her
- ❑ A single migrant worker giving vegetables to a family of migrant workers

JESUS WAS TALKING TO ME

If I give when I have a lot, it's...

better than nothing

nice

lame

sacrifice

But if I give when I don't have much, it's...

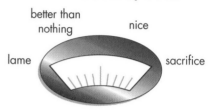

better than nothing

nice

lame

sacrifice

What kinds of things can a teen give that would be a sacrifice?
(Think—don't just write "money")

DARE THE TRUTH

Write three things you could give up for God (be specific) that would be a sacrifice:

Now go back and circle one that you will do this week.

Don't Forget

Read: Luke 22:19–20

WHAT JESUS **SAID**

Jesus wanted his followers to: (Check all that apply.)
- ❑ eat all the time, and drink too!
- ❑ remember him.
- ❑ remember what he did for them.
- ❑ have a ritual that would remind them to remember him
- ❑ throw burger bashes
- ❑ start a ritual that no one really understands

What's this called that Jesus started with the disciples? (Check one)

WHAT JESUS **MEANT**

- ❑ Eucharist
- ❑ Lord's Supper
- ❑ Communion
- ❑ Burger-mania

(Hint: There's not one right answer to this because different churches call it different things!)

Why do you think Jesus wanted the disciples to do this? Couldn't they remember him just by talking about him? Write about that:

JESUS WAS TALKING TO ME

Churches celebrate communion or the Eucharist or the Lord's Supper in lots of different ways. Ask an adult in your church (a parent, a minister, or your youth worker) about the reasons behind the way your church follows this dare. Write a paragraph about it here:

Which of these teens understands Jesus' dare? (Check as many as make sense.)
- ❏ Whenever her church has communion, Marcella tries to spend some time thinking about the sin in her life. Then she asks God for forgiveness and takes the bread and wine (or grape juice) with a sense of amazement for what Jesus did for her.
- ❏ Matthew thinks of communion as a celebration: he loves to use it as a time to thank God for being more powerful than even death and for sending Jesus to earth so Matthew (and other Jesus followers) can be forgiven and know God.
- ❏ Olivia gets totally freaked out about communion. They whole thing seems so weird—all that talk of blood and broken bodies. Ick! She wants to be a good person, so she takes communion like everyone else 'cause—well—she's supposed to.

How often do you follow through on this dare?

Why do you do it?

DARE THE TRUTH

This dare is different than all other dares in this book.
You're going to come up with your own way of applying the dare. Maybe you need to make sure you take part in communion or help prepare it next time your church celebrates it. Or maybe there's another idea you can think of. What can you do?

The Big Dare

Read: John 3:16–18

Thank You Jesus.

WHAT JESUS **SAID**

THE TRUTH

God loves: (More than one might be true, but check what the verse says.)
❑ people ❑ the church ❑ the world ❑ pastrami sandwiches

So he gave:
❑ Jesus ❑ green Jell-O ❑ the Bible ❑ the 10 Commandments

And if we believe in Jesus, then:
❑ we become God's children
❑ we get whatever we want

❑ we get green Jell-O and pastrami sandwiches
❑ we get eternal life

Maybe you've heard this verse all your life—since you were an itty, bitty, little thing. So what are the most important words in this verse? Write four of them here:

WHAT JESUS **MEANT**

THE TRUTH

_____ _____ _____ _____

Then write a couple of sentences about why you chose them:

JESUS WAS TALKING TO ME

What do you believe about Jesus? (Write as many things as you can think of.)

Why is this the ultimate dare?

Have you taken this dare? (Circle one)   Yes   No   I'm not sure

If so, when?

If not, why not?

Choose one of these two gutsy acts:

DARE THE TRUTH

❏ I'm going to take
this dare for the first time: I'm going to believe that Jesus' death on the cross paid the penalty for my sins and makes it possible for me to have a relationship with God. I accept the challenge and put my faith in Jesus.

❏ I already have a relationship with God—I've already accepted this dare. But I don't always live as if I really believe Jesus saved me. So I'm going to apply this dare by taking a risky step of faith and doing something to prove it. (Write that risky step here…)

Live In The Light

Read: John 3:20-21

WHAT JESUS **SAID**

THE TRUTH

If you do bad stuff, you don't like...(Choose one.)
❏ good stuff ❏ light ❏ squid ❏ Jesus

Because light...(Choose one.)
❏ exposes the bad stuff ❏ is the opposite of dark
❏ takes lots of electricity ❏ can blind you

Only those who are committed to _____ are willing to come into the light. (Choose one.)
❏ themselves ❏ God ❏ Ken and Barbie ❏ truth

WHAT JESUS **MEANT**

THE TRUTH

Jesus uses a metaphor here. (Remember, a metaphor is when you use one kind of image to describe something else—like "Mrs. Johnson is a cow.") The metaphor he uses is:
❏ peaches and cream
❏ darkness and light
❏ sin and, um, the opposite of sin

And he uses this metaphor to describe:
❏ the cost of discipleship
❏ the strange ways of the kangaroo
❏ truthfulness and sin

JESUS WAS TALKING TO ME

Light Teens

Rank these students from "most in the light" (4) to "least in the light" (1):

____ Cherie messed up this week—big time. She lied to her mom and dad and got away with it. But even though she knew they would never find out otherwise, she decided to 'fess up and tell them what she'd done—knowing she'd get in big trouble. She just figured that's what living in the light was all about.

____ Candy made a tough choice today: all her friends were going over to someone's house to watch a video. She totally wanted to go—and knew she'd have a great time if she did. But she also knew that they'd be looking at sexy fashion magazines, and she really didn't want to fill her mind with those images. She felt like going along and looking at the magazines would be like walking into the darkness.

____ Conrad is not having a good day—this "living in the light" stuff is *so* hard! His friend Corey wanted to cheat off Conrad's quiz. He always let Corey cheat in the past, and it never seemed like a big deal. But he's been thinking about this "living in the light" stuff, and it just seemed like the opposite of what Jesus would want him to do. Corey's really ticked at Conrad, and he's telling everyone what a jerk he is. Conrad's feeling like staying in the light will not always be easy!

How have you been doing lately at living in the light? (Make a mark on this scale.)

total darkness!   a bit dusky   a bit of light   blinding light!

**Time to get into the light!
Write about an untruth in
your life (a lie you told or some other way you've been living in the
darkness), and write about how you will correct it this week:**

DARE THE TRUTH

How i've been in the dark:	What i'll do to come into the light this week:

Drink Up

Read: John 4:13-14

WHAT JESUS **SAID**

If you're thirsty, you can: (Choose one.)
- ❏ complain
- ❏ get a drink of water
- ❏ stay thirsty

But, sometime later, you'll: (Choose one.)
- ❏ be thirsty again!
- ❏ be hungry!
- ❏ have to pee!

But if you drink in Jesus: (Choose one.)
- ❏ you'll get some super-purified magic water
- ❏ you'll choke
- ❏ you'll never be thirsty again

Circle the correct words or phrases for this paragraph:

WHAT JESUS **MEANT**

The fine folks at Sprite, the beverage company, said it very well: Image is Nothing, Obey Your Thirst! Now, this stuff Jesus is talking about is kinda hard to understand. He starts by talking about [*bottled water, physical thirst, instant coffee*]; but then he starts talking about [*alcohol, soda pop, spiritual thirst*]. It's another one of those [*metaphors, Jesus-isms, guilt trips*]. And he means that as long as we try to fill up on [*no-brand soda, other stuff, dog biscuits*], we'll never be satisfied. Only when we look to Jesus to meet our needs will we be [*fully satisfied, Christians, ice-age mummies*].

THE DARE!

JESUS WAS TALKING TO ME

Which of these are ways to draw Jesus-water from the "eternal life well"?
(Check all that apply.)

- ❑ Pray, and listen to God.
- ❑ Go swimming.
- ❑ Watch for Jesus in other people.
- ❑ Worship.
- ❑ Keep an ice-cube or two in your backpack.
- ❑ Listen during sermons, and do that application thing.
- ❑ Trust Jesus to meet your needs, rather than depending on yourself.
- ❑ Listen to your youth worker, and try to apply his or her teaching to your life
- ❑ Watch for Jesus in your everyday life.
- ❑ Buy stock in a bottled water company.

- ❑ Stop at the drinking fountain all the time.
- ❑ Drink eight glasses of water every day.
- ❑ Never eat anything; just drink a lot.
- ❑ Get into God's Word.

Now go back over that list, and look at the ideas you checked. Put a star next to the ones you do on a regular (at least weekly—daily if possible) basis.

What are some ways that young teens (you, really) try to get your spiritual thirst met, other than the ideas above (things people try, but don't really work)? (Write at least three thoughts.)

Look back over the list at the top of the page again. Did you check any that you didn't put a star next to? (C'mon, we all need to grow in this area.) Choose one you didn't star—one you can do something about—and write about how you'll make it a dare this week:

DARE THE TRUTH

Eat Like a Pig!

Read: John 6:35

WHAT JESUS **SAID**

Jesus said he's like: (Choose one.)

❏ the stars   ❏ God   ❏ bread   ❏ a cosmic Santa Claus

And if you take what he offers, you'll: (Choose one.)

❏ be a super-happy perfect person   ❏ dance a little jig   ❏ never go hungry

WHAT JESUS **MEANT**

Like the last dare, Jesus isn't really talking about: (Choose three.)

❏ Big Macs and fries   ❏ Steak and Eggs   ❏ Bread

He's talking about:

That means you have two choices: (Choose one.)

❏ Rely on other stuff to meet your needs, and never have them met; or rely on Jesus, and have all your needs met.

❏ Starve yourself, or eat a nice healthy meal.

JESUS WAS TALKING

TO ME

Because this dare is so much like the last one (Drink up!), we're going to focus on the last sentence, which says:

❑ "You have seen me and still you do not believe."

❑ "You're such lame followers—I wish you would get your act together."

❑ "I wisheth that thou wouldest be a better person and that thou wouldest eateth more bread."

If we know that Jesus is really able to meet all our needs, how come we continue to try to live life on our own without depending on him? (This is a huge question, one that applies to every single Jesus follower. Spend some time thinking about it; then write what you're thinking.)

Which of these reasons are true for you? (Check all that apply.)

❑ Sometimes I don't think Jesus can really meet my needs.

❑ Sometimes I don't think Jesus knows what's going on in my life.

❑ It's hard to trust Jesus to meet my needs when I can't see him.

❑ Sometimes I just forget that Jesus is there and able to meet my needs.

❑ Sometimes I'm embarrassed by my needs, and I would rather deal with them on my own than bother Jesus.

Name one need you have that you've not been relying on Jesus to meet—

DARE THE TRUTH

one area where you haven't been "feasting on the bread Jesus offers":

Write a prayer asking Jesus to meet that need for you:

Know You're His

Read: John 10:27-28

WHAT JESUS SAID

Jesus calls us: (Choose one.)
- ❏ nerds
- ❏ sheep
- ❏ Christians
- ❏ shepherds

He also says: (Choose one.)
- ❏ If you're not a good sheep, Jesus will make a nice sweater out of your wool!
- ❏ Sheep are really stupid, and they sometimes follow each other off cliffs.
- ❏ You better be careful, or Jesus will trade you to another shepherd.
- ❏ No one can take his sheep away from him.

WHAT JESUS MEANT

The people the Bible was originally written for understood: (Choose one)
- ❏ everything Jesus said
- ❏ sheep and shepherds
- ❏ that they belonged to Jesus and no one else

So they understood that: (Choose one)
- ❏ sheep are one of the stupidest animals on the planet!
- ❏ Jesus would lead them to the best pasture.
- ❏ sheep learn to recognize their shepherd's voice, and follow when they're called.

JESUS WAS TALKING TO ME

Which of the following things can you be totally and completely sure of? (Check all that apply.)

- ❑ my friends staying my friends
- ❑ getting a good job some day
- ❑ that I'll feel good tomorrow
- ❑ my safety at school
- ❑ nothing in my life really changing
- ❑ living where I live as long as I want

- ❑ getting good grades in school
- ❑ having a decent home to live in
- ❑ my health
- ❑ graduating from high school
- ❑ I'll get married someday
- ❑ my parents staying together (if they are)

How many of the items on that list did you check?

none One or more, but I like to believe in things that aren't true

BUT, according to what this verse says, I can be completely sure: (Check all that apply)

- ❑ If I'm a Jesus-follower, I'm guaranteed to stay his.
- ❑ If I've chosen to trust in Jesus, I'm guaranteed a place in heaven.
- ❑ If I've joined the "Jesus-herd," there's nothing I can do that will make him kick me out of it!

DARE THE TRUTH

Since this is a "knowing" dare, the action is a bit different. It's not about what you have to do as much as what you don't have to do. Understanding that "you cannot be snatched from his hand" will make this difference in my life:

Bonus dare: maybe you've never trusted Jesus to be your savior—You've never become one of his sheep. Jesus is daring you to join his herd and know the promise of this dare!

- ❑ I'm already there—I'm in the herd.
- ❑ I'm not sure I'm ready to join the herd.
- ❑ I'm going to take this dare and join the herd for the first time—right now!

Live Forever

Read: John 11:25–26

WHAT JESUS SAID

Jesus said if you believe in him, you'll still: (Choose one)
❏ have homework ❏ get zits ❏ die

But, you'll: (Choose one)
❏ live ❏ get over it ❏ enjoy it

And if you live and believe in him, you'll never: (Choose one)
❏ die ❏ get zits ❏ eat burritos again

WHAT JESUS MEANT

Is this confusing? Yes No

Let's do the math! (Circle answers.)

1. Being human pretty much always ends in X
   X = a. death b. no death

2. But if you're a Jesus-follower, you get Y
   Y = a. eternal life b. eternal separation from God

3. And that means—while you'll die *physically*—you'll never Z
   Z = a. experience eternal death b. eat burritos again

Get it? Yes No Uh, I think so

JESUS WAS TALKING TO ME

It's Saturday night, and you're with your friends hanging out at the mall. Over a Slurpee in the food court, a surprisingly serious conversation starts. It seems Jessica is all worked up about the fact that she's going to die someday (her hamster died the other day, and it got her thinking about death). How does knowing that you're going to live forever influence what you say?

You're talking on the phone with Toben, and out of the blue he asks, "Hey, how come you care about doing good stuff? I mean, you're not perfect! But it seems like you're different from other people." How does knowing that you're going to live forever affect what you say?

You're at a funeral. The person who died is an old person from your church—you didn't really know her very well, so it's not like you're really sad or anything. How does knowing that you're going to live forever affect how you feel about being at a funeral?

Jesus ends this dare by asking, "Do you believe this?" Well...do you?

| No, I don't believe it at all. | I'm struggling to believe it. | I guess I believe it, but it doesn't affect how I live. | I believe it, and it affects everything I do and say. |

If you REALLY believe that you're going to live forever, it WILL affect everything you do and say.

DARE THE TRUTH

What's an area of your life that could change if you accept this dare? Write a couple of sentences about that, and what you can do about it this week:

Die

Read: John 12:24–26

WHAT JESUS **SAID**

Circle the words that go in the blanks:

When a ___(a)___ falls to the ground and ___(b)___, it can ___(c)___. But if it doesn't fall to the ground and ___(b)___, the ___(a)___ will just remain a ___(a)___.

(a)	(b)	(c)
pepperoni pizza	pukes	compete in the Olympics
God follower	chug-a-lugs	produce a bunch of seeds
kernel of wheat	worships God	make God smile
cheese puff	dies	die happy

WHAT JESUS **MEANT**

Jesus isn't really talking about seeds and kernels. (He does that kind of thing a lot, doesn't he?) He's talking about:

❏ Being a good person and developing a system of self-improvement.
❏ Reading your Bible and praying a lot so you can grow in your relationship with God.
❏ Giving up control of your life and having God take control, so that you can really live.
❏ The good ol' farming life: Jesus wants everyone to consider becoming a wheat farmer.

JESUS WAS TALKING TO ME

Here's a mini-dare: read Galatians 2:20 (Yeah, I know you already read a verse today—but you can handle it!) Paul wrote this verse. What does he understand about this dying stuff?

Calvin's parents are always pushing him to do well in school. And he wants to do well—so it's not a real big deal: but he's tired of the reasoning behind it: "so that he can get a good job someday." This morning when Calvin woke up, he prayed, "God, I want to be like a kernel of wheat and die, so I can live."
What did Calvin mean? What difference would it make in his life?

Does this mean Calvin shouldn't try hard to do well in school anymore? Write your thoughts:

In what area of your life do you need to "die" so you can really live? In other words: what part of your life do you hold on to and not give control to God?

DARE THE TRUTH

Write a note to God about that area and what it would mean for you to "die" this week:

Show the Sign

Read: John 13:34–35

WHAT JESUS **SAID**

If you want to be a Jesus-follower, you have to: (Choose one)
- ❑ read the Bible all the time
- ❑ stand on street corner and preach
- ❑ wear an "I'm a Jesus follower" T-shirt
- ❑ love other Jesus followers

The world (people who are not Jesus followers) will be able to tell we're serious about this God stuff when we: (Choose one)
- ❑ put "God Rules" stickers on the back of our cars
- ❑ smile all the time
- ❑ love each other
- ❑ buy Christian music

WHAT JESUS **MEANT**

This is important! Loving other Jesus followers is:
(Choose one.)
- ❑ a command
- ❑ a suggestion
- ❑ an idea
- ❑ an optional thing

Pretend you're a parent with three kids. How do you feel when your kids treat each other like dirt?

We're God's children: How do you think it makes him feel when we don't love each other? (Don't just write a wimpy one-word answer *here*, like *bad*. Take time to think about it, and write a sentence or two.)

How can you show love to other Jesus followers? (Check all that apply.)

❑ Make fun of them.
❑ Don't gossip about them.
❑ Write an encouraging note.
❑ Treat them with respect.
❑ Speak good things about them.
❑ Other:

❑ Smile and be nice.
❑ Annoy them.
❑ Spread lies about them
❑ Spend time together
❑ Don't include them in things you do.
❑ Other:

❑ Trash their stuff.
❑ Support their plans.
❑ Meet their needs.

Make sure you wrote something in the two "other" spaces above.

Are you ever guilty of not treating other Christians with love, as brothers and sisters? (Circle one.)

Yes   No, but I'm a big fat liar (See, I'm lying right now.)

What did Jesus say again? If we love other Christians, what will the result be? (Check one)

❑ We'll get to go to heaven.
❑ God won't make us eat our spinach.
❑ Other people will be able to see that we're Jesus followers.

Let's get lovin'! Think up a creative plan to show love to another Christian whom

DARE THE TRUTH

you've not been very loving toward. (This could be someone from your church, but it doesn't have to be.) Don't wimp out and choose a good friend! Write your plan here:

Now, do it—right now! Come back and check here when you've completed the dare: ❑

(Now keep doing it—keep loving!)

Others First

Read: John 15:12–14

WHAT JESUS **SAID**

Uh-oh, it's another: (Check one)
❑ suggestion ❑ idea ❑ command

That means: (Check one)
❑ I've got to do it—no argument.
❑ I get to decide if it's best for me or not.
❑ Adults have to do it (but not teens).

WHAT JESUS **MEANT**

If a license plate summarized this dare, it might say: (Circle any that apply.)

Heaven
U 1ST

Heaven
WUT I WNT

Heaven
IL GIV 4U

What does it mean to "lay down your life for a friend"? Does Jesus want you to take a bullet for your friend or something? Write about that:

JESUS WAS TALKING
TO ME

Rank these teens in order from the one who's living this dare the least (1) to the one who's living this dare the most (4):

Vicki had plans to go to her aunt's house this weekend—one of her favorite places to be. But just before leaving on Friday, her friend Tasha called and told Vicki how lonely she's been feeling lately. Vicki canceled her plans to visit her aunt (even though she didn't want to) and spent time with Tasha instead. **Rank Vicki:** ____

Bryce gets every trumpet solo in the band—partly because he's good, and partly because the band director never thinks to give the solos to anyone else. Leon, Bryce's friend and also a good trumpet player, asks Bryce if he could have one of the solos for their upcoming concert. Bryce thinks about it and decides to keep all the solos for himself. He thinks, "If Leon's good enough, he'll get a solo on his own merit." **Rank Bryce:** ____

Kaitlyn's family doesn't have much money, and she's stressed about a school dance that's coming up, because she doesn't have anything pretty to wear. Today Kaitlyn was in Kerry's room, and they were talking about the dance. Kerry opened her closet and said: "Kaitlyn, pick anything you want—you can have it." Kaitlyn chose a beautiful dress she could never have afforded—the one Kerry was planning on wearing to the dance. Kerry smiled and let Kaitlyn have the dress. **Rank Kerry:** ____

Jonah and Paul are at the video store trying to choose a game to rent. Jonah's mom told them very clearly they could only choose one. And they're having a hard time agreeing on one. Paul says, "Hey, it's not big deal—I'm cool with getting the one you want." **Rank Paul:** ____

DARE THE TRUTH

Think of a situation where you've been putting your desires in front of a friend's (or family member's) desires. Describe that:

What can you do to "lay down your life" this week in that situation?

Relax

Read: John 16:33

WHAT JESUS **SAID**

Jesus wants you to have: (Check one)
- ❏ peace
- ❏ good grades
- ❏ fun

He promises that: (Check one)
- ❏ you'll never have another problem if you follow him
- ❏ you'll know how to get around every problem you face
- ❏ you'll still have problems in life

But he says to "take heart" because: (Check one)
- ❏ this life is temporary
- ❏ you'll get over it
- ❏ he's more powerful than any problem you'll face

WHAT JESUS **MEANT**

Circle the paragraph that you think best summarizes what Jesus was saying:

I'm frustrated with you sometimes. You're not good enough. I know you try—but you sure fail a lot! Here's the deal: you can experience great peace in your life if you'd just be a better person. And then you won't have so many problems either. You bring them on yourself, you know?

I really want you to experience peace. Now, there's no getting around the fact that you'll have some tough times and problems in your life. But the good news is that I'm more powerful than any of those problems—I'm even more powerful than death. So stick with me!

JESUS WAS TALKING TO ME

Tough question: What does it mean to experience peace in your life?

Which of these is the best definition of the peace Jesus offers us? (Check one)
- ❑ a mellow mood based on circumstances (like, if life is going well or not)
- ❑ a calm easy-going feeling not really based on anything
- ❑ a confidence that comes from knowing Jesus is more powerful than any problem I'll face in life

How much peace to you experience in your life?
(Add a needle to this meter to show your answer.)

not much peace   some peace

no peace at all   perfect peace

Assuming you'd like to experience MORE peace, what do you think keeps you from that experience in your life? (Check all that apply.)
- ❑ I haven't understood this before.
- ❑ I get really stressed about my problem, and I forget that Jesus is more powerful.
- ❑ I'm still not sure Jesus is more powerful than my problems.
- ❑ I don't see the connection (or can't seem to make the connection) between peace and Jesus.
- ❑ Other:

Write a note to Jesus here about a problem you're facing. Ask him to let you experience the peace he wants to give you.

DARE THE TRUTH

Resources from Youth Specialties
www.youthspecialties.com

Ideas Library
Ideas Library on CD-ROM 2.0
Administration, Publicity, & Fundraising
Camps, Retreats, Missions, & Service Ideas
Creative Meetings, Bible Lessons, & Worship Ideas
Crowd Breakers & Mixers
Discussion & Lesson Starters
Discussion & Lesson Starters 2
Drama, Skits, & Sketches
Drama, Skits, & Sketches 2
Drama, Skits, & Sketches 3
Games
Games 2
Games 3
Holiday Ideas
Special Events

Bible Curricula
Backstage Pass to the Bible Kit
Creative Bible Lessons from the Old Testament
Creative Bible Lessons in 1 & 2 Corinthians
Creative Bible Lessons in Galatians and Philippians
Creative Bible Lessons in John
Creative Bible Lessons in Romans
Creative Bible Lessons on the Life of Christ
Creative Bible Lessons on the Prophets
Creative Bible Lessons in Psalms
Wild Truth Bible Lessons
Wild Truth Bible Lessons 2
Wild Truth Bible Lessons—Pictures of God
Wild Truth Bible Lessons—Pictures of God 2
Wild Truth Bible Lessons—Dares from Jesus
Wild Truth Bible Lessons
Wild Truth Bible Lessons 2
Wild Truth Bible Lessons—Pictures of God
Wild Truth Bible Lessons—Pictures of God 2
Wild Truth Bible Lessons—Dares from Jesus

Topical Curricula
Creative Junior High Programs from A to Z,
    Vol. 1 (A-M)
Creative Junior High Programs from A to Z,
    Vol. 2 (N-Z)
Girls: 10 Gutsy, God-Centered Sessions on Issues
    That Matter to Girls
Guys: 10 Fearless, Faith-Focused Sessions on
    Issues That Matter to Guys
Good Sex
The Justice Mission
Live the Life! Student Evangelism Training Kit
The Next Level Youth Leader's Kit
Roaring Lambs
So What Am I Gonna Do with My Life?
Student Leadership Training Manual
Student Underground
Talking the Walk
What Would Jesus Do? Youth Leader's Kit

Drama Resources
Drama, Skits, & Sketches (Ideas Library)
Drama, Skits, & Sketches 2 (Ideas Library)
Drama, Skits, & Sketches 3 (Ideas Library)
Dramatic Pauses
Good Sex Drama
Spontaneous Melodramas
Spontaneous Melodramas 2
Super Sketches for Youth Ministry

Game Resources
Games (Ideas Library)
Games 2 (Ideas Library)
Games 3 (Ideas Library)
Junior High Game Nights
More Junior High Game Nights
Play It!
Screen Play CD-ROM

Discussion Starters

Discussion & Lesson Starters (Ideas Library)
Discussion & Lesson Starters 2 (Ideas Library)
EdgeTV
Every Picture Tells a Story
Get 'Em Talking
Keep 'Em Talking!
Good Sex Drama
Have You Ever...?
Name Your Favorite
Unfinished Sentences
What If...?
Would You Rather...?
High School TalkSheets—Updated!
More High School TalkSheets—Updated!
High School TalkSheets from Psalms and
    Proverbs—Updated!
Junior High-Middle School TalkSheets—Updated!
More Junior High-Middle School
    TalkSheets—Updated!
Junior High-Middle School TalkSheets from Psalms
    and Proverbs—Updated!
Real Kids Ultimate Discussion-Starting Videos:
        Castaways
        Growing Up Fast
        Hardship & Healing
        Quick Takes
        Survivors
        Word on the Street
Small Group Qs

Quick Question Books

Have You Ever...?
Name Your Favorite
Unfinished Sentences
What If...?
Would You Rather...?

Additional Programming Resources

    (also see Discussion Starters)
The Book of Uncommon Prayer
Camps, Retreats, Missions, & Service Ideas
    (Ideas Library)
Creative Meetings, Bible Lessons, & Worship
    Ideas (Ideas Library)
Crowd Breakers & Mixers (Ideas Library)
Everyday Object Lessons
Great Fundraising Ideas for Youth Groups
More Great Fundraising Ideas for Youth Groups
Great Retreats for Youth Groups
Great Talk Outlines for Youth Ministry
Holiday Ideas (Ideas Library)
Incredible Questionnaires for Youth Ministry
Kickstarters
Memory Makers
Special Events (Ideas Library)
Videos That Teach
Videos That Teach 2
Worship Services for Youth Groups

Videos & Video Curricula

Dynamic Communicators Workshop
EdgeTV
The Justice Mission
Live the Life! Student Evangelism Training Kit
Make 'Em Laugh!
Purpose-Driven® Youth Ministry Training Kit
Real Kids Ultimate Discussion-Starting Videos:
        Castaways
        Growing Up Fast
        Hardship & Healing
        Quick Takes
        Survivors
        Word on the Street
Student Underground
Understanding Your Teenager Video Curriculum
Youth Ministry Outside the Lines

Especially for Junior High

Creative Junior High Programs from A to Z, Vol. 1 (A-M)

Creative Junior High Programs from A to Z, Vol. 2 (N-Z)

Junior High Game Nights

More Junior High Game Nights

Junior High-Middle School TalkSheets—Updated!

More Junior High-Middle School TalkSheets—Updated!

Junior High-Middle School TalkSheets from Psalms and Proverbs—Updated!

Wild Truth Journal for Junior Highers

Wild Truth Bible Lessons

Wild Truth Bible Lessons 2

Wild Truth Journal—Pictures of God

Wild Truth Bible Lessons—Pictures of God

Wild Truth Bible Lessons—Dares from Jesus

Wild Truth Journal—Dares from Jesus

Student Resources

Backstage Pass to the Bible: An All-Access Tour of the New Testament

Backstage Pass to the Bible: An All-Access Tour of the Old Testament

Grow for It! Journal through the Scriptures

So What Am I Gonna Do with My Life?

Spiritual Challenge Journal: The Next Level

Teen Devotional Bible

What (Almost) Nobody Will Tell You about Sex

What Would Jesus Do? Spiritual Challenge Journal

Clip Art

Youth Group Activities (print)

Clip Art Library Version 2.0 (CD-ROM)

Academic Resources

Four Views of Youth Ministry & the Church

Starting Right

Youth Ministry That Transforms

Professional Resources

Administration, Publicity, & Fundraising (Ideas Library)

Dynamic Communicators Workshop

Great Talk Outlines for Youth Ministry

Help! I'm a Junior High Youth Worker!

Help! I'm a Small Church Youth Worker!

Help! I'm a Small-Group Leader!

Help! I'm a Sunday School Teacher!

Help! I'm an Urban Youth Worker!

Help! I'm a Volunteer Youth Worker!

Hot Illustrations for Youth Talks

More Hot Illustrations for Youth Talks

Still More Hot Illustrations for Youth Talks

Hot Illustrations for Youth Talks 4

How to Expand Your Youth Ministry

How to Speak to Youth...and Keep Them Awake at the Same Time

Junior High Ministry (Updated & Expanded)

Just Shoot Me

Make 'Em Laugh!

The Ministry of Nurture

Postmodern Youth Ministry

Purpose-Driven® Youth Ministry

Purpose-Driven® Youth Ministry Training Kit

So That's Why I Keep Doing This!

Teaching the Bible Creatively

Your First Two Years in Youth Ministry

A Youth Ministry Crash Course

Youth Ministry Management Tools

The Youth Worker's Handbook to Family Ministry

Digital Resources

Clip Art Library Version 2.0 (CD-ROM)

Great Talk Outlines for Youth Ministry

Ideas Library on CD-ROM 2.0

Screen Play

Youth Ministry Management Tools

Hot Illustrations CD-ROM